THE PENNSYLVANIA DUTCH COUNTRY

Hattie Brunner (1889–1982) is often called "the Pennsylvania German Grandma Moses." Brunner, an antiques dealer by trade, turned to painting late in her life. "Bringing Home Christmas" is one of her typical watercolors. She especially favored snow scenes because she could let the unpainted paper stand in for background. The Christmas theme is popular with the Dutch, who are credited with introducing the Christmas tree into American culture. (Heritage Center Museum of Lancaster County.)

THE PENNSYLVANIA DUTCH COUNTRY

IRWIN RICHMAN

ARCADIA

Copyright © 2004 by Irwin Richman
ISBN 0-7385-2458-1

Published by Arcadia Publishing,
an imprint of Tempus Publishing, Inc.
Charleston SC, Chicago, Portsmouth NH, San Francisco

Printed in Great Britain.

Library of Congress Catalog Card Number: 2003115625

For all general information contact Arcadia Publishing at:
Telephone 843-853-2070
Fax 843-853-0044
E-Mail sales@arcadiapublishing.com
For customer service and orders:
Toll-Free 1-888-313-2665

Visit us on the Internet at http://www.arcadiapublishing.com

CONTENTS

ACKNOWLEDGMENTS

This book has been written for the benefit of the Heritage Center Museum of Lancaster County, an institution devoted, as part of its mission, to preserving and displaying the artifacts of the Pennsylvania Dutch culture. Peter Seibert, director of the Heritage Center Museum, and his staff have helped in collecting many of the illustrations I have used. My thanks go to Wendell Zercher, Kimberly A. Fortney, Sandra Lane, and Sheila Rohrer, all of whom I number among my friends. Three were my graduate students. I am blessed.

As always, the staff and my colleagues at Pennsylvania State University at Harrisburg have been ever helpful. Our library staff is especially wonderful. Our reference librarians, including Greg Crawford, Alan Mays, Eric Delozier, Glenn McGuigan, and Patrick Hall, retrieved arcane information for me and checked many facts, and our inter-library loan librarian, Ruth Runion-Slear, also facilitated my project. Because I am technologically challenged, staff assistants Sue Etters and Cindy Leach typed many letters and e-mails for me, always with professional dispatch and grace. My school directors, Bill Mahar (who has since become our dean) and Simon Bronner; and Patti Mills, the acting dean for Research and Graduate Studies at the Pennsylvania State University at Harrisburg, have once again demonstrated that they give more than lip service to the phrase "faculty development and support." Through their good offices, the typing of my manuscript, which is actually composed in ink on yellow legal pads, has been translated and typed by Linda Seaman. I envy, but have not yet tried to emulate, my hero Harry Potter, who writes on parchment using goose quill pens. The index was prepared by Martha Sachs, special collections librarian, Pennsylvania State University at Harrisburg.

My wife Dr. M. Susan Richman and her extended Pennsylvania Dutch Steigerwalt-Kressley clan have always been very supportive of my interests, especially her mother Florence Caroline Steigerwalt and her late father the Reverend Eugene Oscar Steigerwalt. Our elder son Dr. Alexander Eugene

Acknowledgments

lives in Dutch-influenced country, Union County, where he is a faculty member at Bucknell University. Our younger son Joshua Solomon lives in diaspora, in Alabama, with our southern-born daughter-in-law Kristin Graham Richman and our grandchildren, Benjamin David and Zoë Elizabeth Anne, and is working on his joint M.D. and Ph.D. degrees. This book is for all of them.

The Cottage
Bainbridge, Pennsylvania
December, 2003

Front cover: *Laura Irene Steigerwalt (1883–1961) and Elmer E. Steigerwalt (1881–1953), young teachers, leave on their wedding trip from their hometown of Lehighton, Carbon County, in 1903. They possibly rented the rig from a local livery stable.*

INTRODUCTION

One of the most surprising statistics to emerge from the 2000 census is that more Americans of European stock can trace their ancestry to Germany than to any other old world entity, including the British Islands. Neither England nor Ireland sent more of their sons and daughters to this shore than did the Germanic peoples. This immigration began during the first half of the seventeenth century and, except for the times of World Wars I and II, has been almost continuous—sometimes as a flood, at other times as a trickle.

German influences are everywhere around us. They are more pervasive than mere sauerkraut, and mostly they are assumed to be simply "American." Many aspects of our culture, from architecture to food and drink and amusement parks, are German influenced. The Brooklyn Bridge, for example, a premier American icon, was designed by a German-born and educated American citizen, John Augustus Roebling (1806–1869), who was so proud of his new land that he named his son, who eventually completed the bridge, George Washington Roebling. Other German Americans designed New York's George Washington Bridge and California's sensational Golden Gate Bridge. It can be truly said that "Germans bridged America." The influence of the Bauhaus school of German architecture has re-shaped our urban and suburban landscape with the slab-like and box-like buildings known as the "International style." Several of the most important of these German architects, including Richard Neutra (1892–1970), Walter Gropius (1883–1969), and Ludwig Mies van der Rohe (1886–1969), would become American citizens.

Where would American cuisine be without the hamburger or the frankfurter—both named for German cities? They are archetypal American foods. Could McDonald's or Burger King exist without the burger? What would an excursion to the ballpark be without an overpriced hot dog? What would we grill for our Fourth of July picnics? In terms of consumption, our favorite and most democratic alcoholic beverage is beer, and while many cultures make beer, including the English, as William L. Dounard's *Dictionary of the History of American Brewing and Distilling Industries* points out:

> lager beer, introduced by German immigrants in the 1840s, was lighter, more effervescent, and more highly hopped than the English beers. Also, the fermentation process utilized a special yeast that settled at the bottom of the vats, and brewers "lagered," or stored, the beer for a time as fermentation proceeded. Modern lager beer, making up more than 90 percent of all beer consumed [in America], is more gently hopped, a bit lower in alcoholic content, and lighter and drier than its nineteenth-century counterpart. Conversely, today's ales contain a greater quantity of hops and are heavier than lager.

The German-inspired beer industry grew most vigorously during the 1850s when breweries increased in number from 431 in 1850 to an astounding 1,269 in 1860. New York and Pennsylvania led the nation in brewing, but migration into the Northwest Territory states such as Illinois, Indiana, Michigan, Ohio, and Wisconsin also led many brewers west. German brewers would later move to Missouri, Colorado, and Texas—indeed, wherever there were Germans in the population. Among the hundreds of German-born brewers who founded the industry in America's largest cities and many small towns were several whose family names have become synonymous with beer: Eberhard Anheuser, Adolph Busch, Valentine Blatz, Adolph Herman Joseph Coors, Frederick Miller, Bernhard Stroh, Joseph Schlitz, Frederick Pabst, Christian Schmidt, and David Yuengling. Other beer makers' brand names reflected their German roots. Samuel Liebmann's beer was sold as "Rheingold."

The favorite American sweet is chocolate or anything chocolate-flavored, and here again the Germans are important. For most Americans, "Hershey" and chocolate are synonymous. Milton Snavely Hershey (1857–1945) quite literally introduced chocolate to mainstream America. The descendant of Germanic ancestors, Hershey changed America's food habits and that deed made him a very rich man. Hershey, Pennsylvania, became known as "Chocolate Town, USA" with its main street, Chocolate Avenue, lined with street lights representing wrapped and unwrapped Hershey Kisses. Following Hershey's lead, Central Pennsylvania became America's chocolate capital. Wilbur's, which primarily manufactures chocolate for confectioners, is still headquartered in Lititz. Its most well known retail candy is Wilbur Buds, which many chocolate fanciers prefer to the more widely known Hershey Kiss. Klein's Chocolate (now part of Mars, Inc.) is in nearby Elizabethtown.

When Americans are ready for recreation, one of their favorite places is a theme park, and the name "Disney" often comes to mind first. And while the Disney empire was founded on a mouse, it owes a great debt to German culture. Disneyland and Walt Disney World are among the most popular tourist destinations in the United States, and their featured fairytale castles (which also exist near Tokyo and Paris) are Germanic in inspiration. The Germanic mythic world of the brothers Grimm (Jacob Ludwig Carl, 1785–1863, and Wilhelm Carl, 1786–1859) has been very good to Walt Disney Enterprises, and the visions of their popular castles owe a great debt to a German monarch, Ludwig II of Bavaria (1846–1886). Known to many of his subjects as Mad King Ludwig, the monarch was in fact an aesthete very much influenced by the romance of the Germanic past. Ascending to the throne at eighteen in 1865, he was a supporter and devotee of opera composer Richard Wagner (1813–1883), whose celebrations of German mythology he adored. As king, Ludwig erected several extravagant palaces that threatened to bankrupt Bavaria. The most famous was Neuschwanstein, built between 1869 and 1886 on a high crag. Celebrating a Germanic mythic past, it was the quintessential fairytale abode, until the Disney versions perhaps improved on it. Neuschwanstein's site, however, has never been matched.

Other American never-never worlds of destination amusement parks often use German references—sometimes explicitly, sometimes more obliquely. Most German is Schlitterbahn Waterpark Resort in the Texas Hill Country. Sherrie Brammall, Schlitterbahn's communications director, writes, "Our original intent was to reflect the German cultural heritage of New Braunfels." But American pop culture intervened: "as the park has evolved over the past two decades, there is not really one consistent architectural style." Brammall also notes, "While our landmark castle is fashioned after the Bergfried Tower at Solms Castle in Braunfels, Germany, I'm afraid our architecture might fall under the heading of 'fractured German influence.' "

At Busch Gardens you actually can visit a smorgasbord of cultures: "Ireland Forever," "Bella Italiana," "Merry Old England," "Bonnie Scotland," "Vive la France," as well as "Do Deutschland." Should you choose the German experience, you are invited to "Get out the Lederhosen, and get ready for Rhinefeld—where the Big Bad Wolf® takes you screaming through the trees and . . . then relax on a Rhine River Cruise through the heart of Germany." You should, of course, expect to "devour your weight in schnitzel," which can be accomplished at "Das Festhaus," which serves up "German sausage, red cabbage and hot potato salad."

Staying in Pennsylvania Dutchland, you can visit HersheyPark and cavort with Hershey candy characters, or visit Lancaster's Dutch Wonderland, now also operated by Hershey Estates, which is replete with many pseudo German references.

Many Americans know about the Pennsylvania Dutch who are, of course, really German, and the German flavor of Milwaukee, but how many know that New York City was known as Kleindeutshland, "Little Germany," or of the existence of the Nebraska or the Texas Germans? George Fenwick Jones's *The Georgia Dutch: From the Rhine and Danube to the Savannah, 1733–1783* documents a little known southern group. Traditional history emphasizes the British Island homogeneity of the South. The existence of Savannah's Lutheran Church of the Ascension whose congregation was founded in 1743, tells a different story. Place names like Berlin and Hanover in New Hampshire are testimony to some non-Yankee roots in New England, as well.

In 2004, for Americans the question of who is German is very easy to answer. A German is simply a citizen of Germany. To the contemporary German, the question is more complex. They recognize Germany as a political entity, of course, but they also factor in Germans as a racial and cultural group as well. Hence, descendants of Germans who emigrated to Russia at the behest of Tzarina Catherine the Great (who reigned from 1762–1796), and who have maintained their Germanic communities and identities into the third millennium, remain Germans and, as such, can return to the Fatherland and reclaim citizenship. Someone who is a resident in Germany is not German, even if they and their parents were born in Germany, if they are not of German stock. An issue in today's Germany is what to do about the children and grandchildren of Turkish "guest workers" who entered Germany by the tens of thousands during Germany's post–World War II economic boom.

In the American context, who is German is more vague and amorphous, especially when you remember that no such country as "Germany" existed as a political entity until 1870. While the history of Germanic peoples can be traced back in Europe over millennia, we are only concerned with their history as it relates to the evolution of the American colonies and the United States in particular.

Today in Europe, there are two countries where German is the official language—Germany and Austria. In a third country, Switzerland, German is one of three major official languages (along with French and Italian), but it is the dominant one. Other countries continue to house German-speaking minorities—with more or less grace. The borders of modern Germany and Austria are twentieth century products—and both are remnants of the Holy Roman Empire of the German People, an important ghost of the Roman Empire that existed, on paper at least, until 1806, and the Austro-Hungarian Empire, which collapsed after World War I.

As a result of political realignments, imperial visions, imperial decay, and emigration, there are German enclaves throughout Central and Eastern Europe, outside of the borders of modern day Germany or Austria. For example, the Sudatenland over which World War II began is again a part of the modern Czech Republic, Silesia is now in Poland.

As complex as the question of who and what is German, the issue of who is a German Jew is even more complex. To the Nazis, the concept of the German Jew was an oxymoron, but Jews have been part of the Germanic saga for over 1,000 years. Before the rise of Hitler's Third Reich, many Jew residents in Germany and Austria considered themselves to be German or Austrian first. German Jewry emigrated into many of the areas where German political hegemony existed. Culturally, Jews are divided into two major groups: the Sephardim, who derive from the Mediterranean East and Spain, and the Ashkenazim, who derive from Germanic areas. Ashkenaz is the ancient Jewish name for Germany. Ashkenazim often spoke Yiddish, but many were also fluent in German and they commonly looked upon German, not Ashkenazic, as their culture and to Judaism as their religion. One branch of the author's family, for example, traces its roots to Galicia in what is now Poland, but was in modern times part of the Austro-Hungarian empire. The immediate family names are not the easily recognizable Jewish names of other portions of Eastern Europe like Lebowitz or Slutsky, but the very Germanic Schwebel and Brinis. German Jews, along with German Protestants and Catholics, have been very influential in the impact that German culture has had on America.

The earliest Germans to settle in what is now the United States were probably Palatine Germans who settled in the Dutch colony of New Netherlands from 1630. By the time of the British conquest of the Dutch colonies in 1664 and the subsequent renaming of "New York," there were probably more Palatine Germans than Holland Dutch people in the former New Netherlands. Early travelers' accounts throughout the Hudson Valley are replete with descriptions of the German presence, and geographic place names that survive like Rhinecliff and Rhinebeck on the bank of the Hudson River, often called "The American Rhine," attest to their presence. During the reign of Queen Anne of England (1702–1720), Palatine Germans were settled by the Crown in New York's Mohawk Valley. Many emigrated to Pennsylvania, but town names like Palatine Bridge, New York, remain.

While the first Germans arrived in Pennsylvania in 1683, the premier great influx of Germans into the colonies came in the period between the 1730s and the 1770s as a result of economic dislocations in the Palatine. Most settled first in Pennsylvania. Subsequently, large numbers of Germans emigrated because of the dislocations of the Napoleon Wars. Economic hard times in the 1830s sent others to the new American nation. Most of these early immigrants were farmers, artisans, and shopkeepers. A few were adventurers.

In the 1840s, waves of revolution swept Europe and especially the numerous German states. When most of these uprisings were quelled in 1848, tens of thousands of additional Germans emigrated. Many were the usual economic refugees, but others were intellectuals and professionals whose liberal views made it dangerous to remain at home. They have come to be known as the "48ers." A number were Jews and this period also marks the first significant Jewish immigration into the United States.

THE PENNSYLVANIA DUTCH COUNTRY

As Germany was unified into a modern state under the leadership and military might of the Prussian Kaiser Wilhelm I (1797–1886) and his "Iron Chancellor" Count Otto von Bismark (1815–1898), culminating in 1870, other Germans fled. As the new German state developed, more dislocations forced more Germans to emigrate. The effects of ever rising militarism up to World War I sent others migrating. Germany's depression after its defeat in World War I sent more out. The rise of the Nazi regime in the 1930s emptied Germany of many of its most promising intellectuals: artists and architects—Christians as well as Jews—many of whom came to America. After World War II, most German immigrants chose to keep a low profile about their national origin until the 1960s. Since then, there has been a regular, but small trickle of Germans who continue to emigrate.

It should also be observed that many Germans leaving their homelands over this great span of time have emigrated to many other areas of the Americas as well as to what became the United States. Canada, Mexico, pre-Castro Cuba, Paraguay, Chile, Argentina, and Brazil were important destinations. Brazil's great landscape architect, Roberto Burle Marx (1909–1994), for example, is of German descent, as is Oscar Niemeyer (*b.* 1907), the quintessential Brazilian modernist and designer of his nation's capital city, Brasilia. After World War II, many unrepentant Nazis found refuge in various countries in Latin America.

Remnants of recognizable German cultures are visible in many areas of the United States. For example, there are more Amish in Indiana than in Pennsylvania; Milwaukee celebrates its beer and sausage tradition; and the Hutterites, about 22,000 strong and living in about 100 colonies dispersed on the Northwestern plains, keep rigidly to the language and customs of their sixteenth-century forebears. But it is only in Pennsylvania Dutch Country that you find the whole range of German descendants—church people and sectarians, Protestants, Catholics, and Jews—people whose ancestors came here in the 1680s, the nineteenth, or twentieth century, and recent immigrants all living their culture in its infinite varieties. The Pennsylvania Dutch stand out distinctly among the other German American cultures of our endlessly diverse nation.

Chapter One

DUTCH COUNTRY AND ITS PEOPLE

The German presence in Pennsylvania began at an extraordinarily early date, in 1683, when a group of Mennonites created a settlement near Philadelphia that would later be called "Germantown." Germantown, which was eventually absorbed into the City of Philadelphia in the nineteenth century, would have a long and distinguished history as an independent community and as a city neighborhood, as part of William Penn's vision for a "Greene Country Towne." William Penn (1644–1718), the social and political radical, the son of Admiral Sir William Penn (1621–1670), a distinguished naval officer knighted by King Charles II, was a Quaker. Despite his family status, the younger William was subjected to harassment against which his wealth allowed him to defend himself. His less well-to-do brethren were not as lucky. Penn was determined to help them to find sanctuary. As a man of his time, he looked toward the new Eden—America.

First, in 1675, he had become one of the proprietors of West New Jersey, where Quakers were encouraged to settle, but the colony was to be mainly populated and ruled by Anglicans—the Church of England establishment. The Penn family had been strong supporters of the monarch and had helped finance Charles II's restoration to the throne in 1660. Admiral Penn loaned the monarch a huge sum of money. Cash-starved Charles II owed the Admiral's estate 16,000 pounds. Poor in money, Charles was rich in claims to territory in America. To satisfy his debt, he made William Penn's dream come true. In 1681, he granted a multimillion-acre colony, which he named "Pennsylvania" in honor of the admiral, to William Penn as proprietor. A proprietor could prosper from his colony only as much as the colony would prosper. First and foremost, the colony needed a transplanted European population. The new colony had fewer than a thousand Swedes and Hollanders, a few hundred Englishmen, and thousands of Native Americans, whose numbers had been greatly reduced because of smallpox and measles inadvertently introduced by the first European settlements. Penn encouraged Quakers to emigrate, and eventually thousands responded, but he realized these would not be enough. A shrewd early-day real estate developer, Penn, through a series of writings, encouraged German Quakers and other sectarians to emigrate to his "Noble Experiment." More painfully persecuted than Quakers in England, they responded, and Germantown was founded as a beachhead for the tens of thousands of Germans, church people, and sectarians who would immigrate into Pennsylvania by 1800. It is from these seventeenth and eighteenth-century immigrants that the Pennsylvania Dutch, the Persistent Minority, are descended.

If the Pennsylvania Dutch are German in origin, why are they called "Dutch?" It is a question of semantics. The author married into an extensive, purebred Pennsylvania German family whose forebears arrived in America in the 1760s and settled in what would become Lehigh, Schuylkill, and Carbon Counties where they would live, as many continue to live, for almost 250 years. Settlements were often rural and isolated with few surnames. Three of Mary Susan Steigerwalt's (Richman's) grandparents were born with the Steigerwalt surname. The fourth grandparent had Steigerwalt ancestry! The author's father-in-law, the Reverend Eugene Oscar Steigerwalt (1905–1994), a Lutheran minister, was expected, until the outbreak of World War II, to conduct one service a month in German. He gloried in being able to speak dialect German "Pennsylvania Dutch" or "Dutch" and he would proudly proclaim himself a "Dutchman," and, indeed, most Pennsylvania Germans comfortably and confidently use the "Dutch" identifier.

Others felt differently. Bucks County artist and art school founder Walter Emerson Baum (1884–1956), like Pastor Steigerwalt, was born of German ancestry, but he hated "Dutch" and insisted on "German," only yielding to "Dutch" during the xenophobic days of World War II. Europe had its Plattdeutsch, the lowlands near the sea including the modern Dutch of Holland, and its Hochdeutsch, the modern Germany. "Deutsch" is easily corrupted into "Dutch." The term "Pennsylvania German," is a late nineteenth-century identifier that a scholarly world introduced to delineate these unique Americans. The commonplace definition of who is considered Pennsylvania Dutch or German, as suggested earlier, is that they are descendants of the complex, mostly German-speaking peoples who arrived in America before 1800. Like all definitions, in practice, it allows for a little elasticity to admit saints and omit sinners.

Within the walls of "Wyck," an elegant, extensively remodeled grand home in Germantown, are remnants of a small house built by Hans Milan, an original Mennonite settler of the area *c.* 1690, possibly making it the oldest surviving house in Pennsylvania. For nine generations, Wyck was the home of the Wistar-Haines family. The house's present appearance was attained in 1824 when it was enlarged and remodeled by architect William Strickland (1708–1854), who turned it into a gentleperson's retreat, often obscuring its Germanic past.

Germantown contains the oldest Mennonite meeting house in America. By the mid-eighteenth century, it was a prosperous community of productive farms and industries, including the pioneering Rittenhouse paper mill. Germantown became famous as a center of the manufacture of woolen stockings, which were widely known in the colonies and in post colonial America. An area of great beauty, Germantown, just 6 miles from the center of the colonial city of Philadelphia, would become the site of country homes of that city's elite. James Logan (1674–1751), William Penn's secretary, who for years actually ran the colony, built "Stenton," which is now a museum, as is the Chew family's great house, "Cliveden," on whose lawn part of the Battle of Germantown was fought during the American Revolution. When the devastating yellow fever epidemic of 1793 hit Philadelphia, President George Washington and his family took refuge from the pestilence in Germantown, at the Deshler-Morris house, now also a museum.

When the railroad arrived in Germantown in the 1840s, the town became one of America's first railroad suburbs and a center of horticulture spurred on, in part, by the many gentlemen estate owners in the neighborhood. The marvelous vine Wisteria was named for Dr. Casper Wistar (1761–1818), whose roots were in Germantown. A noble Wisteria vine thrives at the Wistar ancestral home, "Grumblethorpe."

Today's Germantown is a diverse neighborhood, parts of it blighted, but it is, especially in spring, ablaze with horticultural fireworks— dogwoods, cherries, and azaleas in profusion—and its streets are mostly tree lined. It is as close to Penn's vision of a "Greene Country Towne" that Philadelphia has to offer.

Philadelphia itself had many German residents, and by mid-eighteenth century, German was heard as often as English in the city. Benjamin Franklin and many of his colleagues were afraid that German, rather than English, would become the colony's official language. But Philadelphia's great success as an economic hub and, on the eve of the Revolution, as the second largest city in the Empire after London ensured the domination of English. And while the German presence indelibly marked Philadelphia's palate (scrapple and pretzels are both German in origin), parts of rural Pennsylvania would retain their strong Germanic flavor into the twenty-first century. This rural area is what is today celebrated as "Dutch Country." It includes parts of Bucks and Montgomery Counties to the east and north of Philadelphia, as well as Lehigh, Schuylkill, Snyder, Union, and Carbon Counties; but its heart is in the counties of South Central Pennsylvania: Berks, Lebanon, Dauphin, Northampton, Lancaster, and York. Bordering counties, including Cumberland and Perry, also have Dutch residents. The names of the counties are mostly English; "Schuylkill," however, is derived from the Dutch, and "Dauphin" is French in origin. In the eighteenth century and well into the nineteenth century, these counties, with their English-named cities of Reading, Lancaster, York, Allentown, Bethlehem, and Harrisburg, were largely populated with the Pennsylvania Dutch. There are still many places where people speak with a noticeable Dutch accent. The landscape in Dutch country is dotted with many smaller communities and townships whose names reflect the Germanic character of their early settlers and present inhabitants: Hamburg, Heidleburg, Strasburg, Knauers, Berlin, Reinholds, Myerstown, Wormelsdorf, and Stouchsburg are a small sample.

Just who are the Pennsylvania Dutch? The answer is surprisingly complex. First and foremost, it is important to remember that the modern country called Germany did not exist until 1870. What is today Germany was many states and principalities, and in a world of different political boundaries, we discover that the Germans who immigrated into Pennsylvania were mostly from what is now Germany, but also that some of the Pennsylvania Germans, or Pennsylvania Dutch, are not even German in origin.

Dutch Country and its People

The largest number of Germans came from the Palatinate, die Pfalz, the region near Heidelberg. Many others came from Alsace, which is, of course, now part of France. A visit to an Alsatian folk museum in France is like visiting a collection of Pennsylvania Dutch artifacts, and Alsatian cooking was widely influential on Pennsylvania Dutch cuisine. There is even an Alsace Township in Berks County.

The vast majority of these pre–1800 immigrants were Lutherans and members of the German Reformed Church (now the United Church of Christ) who came here because they were economically stressed. They were part of a seventeenth- and eighteenth-century human tragedy that forced hundreds of thousands of Germans to emigrate to Holland, to England, to Russia, and to the American colonies. They fled lands decimated by wars that raged for decades. Included among them were a smattering of Catholics and Jews. Except for the tiny number of Jews, they came primarily for economic reasons.

After the Edict of Nantes was revoked in 1685, Protestants living in France had to flee for their lives. A number of Huguenots, as they were called, moved into the Palatinate; and when economic conditions there deteriorated, many emigrated with their hosts to the New World where they were absorbed into the dominant Pennsylvania German culture. Other Huguenots immigrated directly from hiding places in France itself or other host countries. The Dutch names Zeller, Greiner, and Deturk, among others, are French Protestant in origin. One group of Palatinate Huguenots traveled first to Holland and then immigrated into the Hudson Valley of New York, founding the settlement of Nieu Pfalz, or "New Paltz."

Smaller church groups and the sectarians are also more cosmopolitan than one would expect. The Schwenkfelders come from Silesia, which is now Poland. Schwenkfelder culture today centers around Pennsburg, which predictably is near Schwenksville, Montgomery County. The Schwenkfelder library, archives, and museum are well worth visiting. The Moravians, a German church with Reformation roots, had its beginnings in what is now the Czech Republic before moving into Germany and sending numerous members to America. Many of these Pennsylvania Dutch are really Czech or even Slovak in background. The Moravians center their faith on missionary efforts and they emigrated for two reasons: to attempt to unify all the diverse Christian denominations in the New World, and to convert the Native Americans. Their results were mixed. The Moravians are proud of the fact that over 90 percent of their members today are in third world countries. The Moravians founded several communities in Pennsylvania, the most successful of which are Lititz (named for Lidice in the Czech Republic), Nazareth, and Bethlehem. All have interesting histories and old world charm in spots. Known for their culture, the Moravians introduced the music of Haydn and Bach to America. Beginning with its custom of having a trombone quartet play from the church tower on Christmas eve, Bethlehem became associated in culture with Christmas. Widely known as "The Christmas City," it is now a tourist destination in the holiday season for its Christmas Mart, its lights, its concerts, and its Putz (or creche).

When most outsiders hear the phrase "Pennsylvania Dutch," they conjure images of the Amish and the Mennonites. These archetypical Pennsylvania Dutch of popular imagination have their roots in Alsace, but most of them immigrated to America from the German-speaking cantons or states of Switzerland. A small number of Mennonites also emigrated from Holland. Unlike the Lutherans and the Reformed Church members, the sectarians came here primarily for religious freedom. The worst of the persecutions these peoples endured is chronicled in a seventeenth-century book, *Het bloedig toonel of Martelaers Spiegel*, or the *Martyrs Mirror*, still important to their faith. *Martyrs Mirror*, printed in Ephrata in Lancaster County in 1748, was the largest book printed in the American colonies.

Some Mennonites and the Amish stand out today because of their dress. By tradition, Mennonites dressed modestly, and until the later nineteenth century and the spread of mail order catalogs, most rural people—church people, Mennonites, or Amish—all dressed pretty much alike. When fashion reached the countryside, a cry went up in Plain circles for modesty. Among the Mennonites, this was usually interpreted into long-sleeved, long-skirted dresses for women, often in subdued colors with small prints. Mennonite women almost always wore a prayer veil or bonnet in public—usually a white or black starched garment worn on top of the head. Men's formal attire eschewed collars, and jackets lacked lapels. Mennonite men did not wear mustaches, which these conscientious objectors connected with militarism. Plain garb is worn less and less among the Mennonites, and today it is not uncommon to see very incongruous sights: a wealthy, diamond-encrusted, stylish lady in a full-length mink coat wearing a prayer veil. Perhaps more jarring is the teenage girl in mini-skirt or hot pants and, again, a prayer veil. Many Mennonite men wear simple sports shirts, open at the collar, and dark slacks. A contemporary Mennonite banker or real estate developer, however, can be seen wearing Hugo Boss or Armani and a power tie.

The Amish, who broke from the Mennonites in the seventeenth century because of the Mennonite's then perceived laxity, are very strict about their garb, which is a stylized version of early nineteenth-century country dress. Amish garb is uniform by community. The Amish prize conformity above all. Amish women wear dresses of red, blue, or greens, and always an apron (to show their readiness for work), and a prayer veil (at home, they might just wear a kerchief). Black stockings complete their attire. A heavy black shawl might be used in winter. Men wear black trousers, always supported by suspenders, never a belt; a white or, less commonly, a colored shirt; and a lapel-less jacket. In winter, men wear black broad-brimmed felt hats. In summer, straw hats are worn. Like their Mennonite brethren, they do not grow mustaches. Amish children dress like miniature versions of their parents. Much Amish and Mennonite clothing is homemade; however, many stores, even department stores, have "Plain Clothes" for their Plain clientele. Amish and Mennonite attire is available off the rack in the heart of the Dutch country.

The Amish are trilingual. They speak English to outsiders, Pennsylvania Dutch among themselves, and high German in their prayers. Today, because of their high birth rate (an average of 7.8 children per family), the Old Order Amish is the fastest growing religious group in America. They are not immune to change. Indeed, most Amish youth, before they are baptized as adults, usually before marriage, experiment with the outside world and have cars and wild drinking parties. Once in the church, they leave these habits. Today, many Amish women favor black athletic shoes, and it is always incongruous seeing Amish kids on inline skates just down the road from their brethren traveling by horse and buggy.

THE PENNSYLVANIA DUTCH COUNTRY

The largely Germanic "Dutch" culture that evolved in Pennsylvania is distinctive. Before World War II, the German government, under the Nazi regime, actively attempted to form pro-Axis Bunden (political organizations) among Americans of German descent. Their efforts completely failed among the Pennsylvania Dutch who felt, and feel, absolutely no sense of loyalty to the modern presumed fatherland. The organizers had much more success with the descendants of later immigrants. Reading, in the heart of Dutch country, attracted many late nineteenth- and early twentieth-century German immigrants, and it became a flourishing center of Nazi sympathy—but not among the traditional, historic residents.

Along with the Spanish of the American Southwest, the Pennsylvania Dutch have nurtured and maintained a unique folk culture that has transcended centuries while interacting with and reacting to the dominant culture. The media of the twentieth century, radio and television especially, have had baleful effects on the natural, organic maintenance of both of these cultures. Today, however, there are many scholars and laymen devoted to the preservation of Dutch culture, which has had a surprisingly expansive effect on American culture at large. E-mail and the Web have helped as links aiding to keep the culture alive and passing on interesting tales. One link: Abraham Lincoln was born in a log cabin; the cabin was built using German log technology. Surprised? Remember that Lincoln's grandfather grew up in Berks County, Pennsylvania—cheek to jowl with the Germans. The log cabin is as American as apple pie—another German contribution to wider American culture. Pie is available in a broad range of variations and it is not always recognized for what it is. Dutch culture can also be chamaeleon-like.

There is an old story about a tourist stopping his car at Amos Zook's gasoline station in Wormelsdorf and asking him, "Where are the Pennsylvania Dutch?" The answer: they are all around you.

Chapter Two

THE DUTCH LANDSCAPE

Culture has shaped the landscape of the Dutch country. While the region certainly has its share of the same strip malls and generic housing developments that deface and attempt to homogenize much of America, there are still substantial areas where the region's distinctiveness shines through, but you must be attuned to read the unwritten cultural messages.

First and foremost, the Dutch have been an agricultural people, and agriculture remains the dominant industry in much of the region. The farms, their layouts, and their buildings are all distinctive. And in various counties, "Century Farms" (farms that have remained in single-family ownership for 100 years or more) are noted and celebrated. There even are numerous farms that have remained in family ownership for over 200 years. The Dutch are a conservative people who value tradition and stability. As you drive down roads in agricultural Dutch country, note that for the most part, houses and barns are built on an east-west axis with the house and barn facing south. Additionally, the farm complex usually faces a road or lane. If a thoroughfare is missing, it was once there. It is theorized that the buildings are on axis because in Europe, houses and barns were often attached and, indeed, there is evidence to suggest that the connected house-barn, hofhaus, was used in Pennsylvania. In what is believed to be the first house in Bethlehem, Moravian leader Nikolaus Ludwig von Zinzindorf (1700–1760) wrote on Christmas Eve in 1740 that he went into the next room "to tell the beasts of the birth of Our Lord," informing us that he was in a barn-house. Census records reveal that house-barns continued to be occupied until the late nineteenth century in some Pennsylvania German areas.

Having buildings face south is commonsensible—buildings facing south are easier to heat. Curiously, too many of the houses have two front doors. And while many farm houses, as well as those in small towns, have been covered in some unsympathetic material like aluminum or plastic siding, most basic house forms remain very identifiable.

Like the Swedes and the English who preceded them into Pennsylvania, the Germans brought with them notions of construction and space usage from Europe. Early houses were half timbered, log, or masonry. The most common floor plan of these houses was a three-room plan common to much of central Europe, but used almost exclusively by Germanic settlers and their descendants in America. The flurküchehaus was customarily divided into three living spaces. The largest of these was the kitchen, or küche, which occupied approximately one-third to slightly less than one-half of the total floor plan. The front door of the house, very often a double articulated, or "Dutch door," generally opened into the küche, which traditionally ran the entire length of the house. In very rare instances, the rear of the küche was divided off into a small chamber or kammerle, which could be used for sleeping or storage, or both. The staircase to the loft above or the second floor was usually narrow and encased and was placed along the wall to the right of the doorway and opposite the fireplace. The cellar stairs, if any, were usually located under these stairs. There might also be a bulkhead door leading to the cellar from outside. A large stone fireplace was placed in the center of the room's left-hand wall. Customarily, the entire stack was in the kitchen. On the chimney wall and usually facing the staircase was a door leading into the stove room, or stube, which usually occupied about two-thirds of the house's remaining space. Opening from the back of the stube was the bedchamber, or kammer.

The küche, or kitchen, was the food preparation center of the house and more. Traditionally, it was the only room in the house where a fire was kept burning continually. In winter, it was often the only warm room in the house. The large hearth openings in many German kitchens are often misunderstood today. Huge fires were never built in these fireplaces; rather, part of the hearth was used like a modern range. Several fires would be kept going for the requirements of what was being cooked: a lively fire for boiling a large pot, a few glowering embers to keep a small pot's contents warm. Part of the large fireplace was used to store several days' worth of firewood. The dry heat from the hearth fire would complete the drying process so that the wood was ready to burn. In some large fireplaces, caged hens were housed to provide the family with a few fresh eggs. It was Odorous, of course, but people had sensibilities different from those of our deodorant enhanced times.

Some fireplaces were fitted with raised hearths to ease the cook's labors. Interestingly, the Germans never used andirons in their fireplaces. Many fireplaces were equipped with adjustable swinging iron cranes for easing the dangerous work of moving large kettles of boiling liquid. In the age of the open hearth, which in some areas of the Pennsylvania German heartland lasted into the twentieth century, scaldings and burns were a major cause of disability and death among women and children. At the back of the fireplace, against the area where fires usually burned, an iron fire back was often installed. This served a dual purpose: to protect the masonry of the chimney stack and to radiate heat as the fire cooled. An opening in the rear wall of another area of the back led into an iron or masonry stove that heated the stube.

Opposite the fireplace, an L-shaped bench was often built into the far corner of the room. During meals, a table, usually the same one on which meals were prepared, was moved into this corner. Everyone except the father or an honored guest would sit on these built-in benches or a movable one used alongside the table. The single chair was, of course, the seat of honor.

A very important ancillary part of the kitchen was the bake oven, which traditionally was constructed outside the house, convenient to the kitchen entrance. A small open shed kept firewood dry and protected the baker. Fires were built in the ovens themselves to heat the walls. When the fire died down, the ashes were raked out and baking could begin. In the pre-thermometer days, women developed many ways of determining when the temperature was right for baking. These included floating a feather in the oven, placing one's arm in the oven and counting, or spitting, on the oven bottom to see how the moisture beaded. Old customs died hard. Educator Nancy Risser recalls that when her maternal grandmother went to live with her very fashionable and upscale daughter and her husband in the 1920s, in an exclusive Harrisburg suburb, she insisted that a bake oven be built "out back" for her use.

Water was very important to a household. The most desirable water source was a nearby reliable spring or a dug well. Often buildings would be constructed over a channeled spring. These "spring houses" were used to store perishables as well as to protect the water source. Lacking a spring, hand-dug wells were often used. German Swiss houses were often built over a spring—the spring ran through the basement. This provided an indoor water source and a primitive refrigerator. A special insulated ceiling made of mud- and straw-wrapped laths kept the cellar cool and helped to keep the upper rooms dry. The question is often asked today about what happened when the spring flooded. The answer is simple: it just flooded; there were no gas or electrical mechanisms to be damaged. Owners of German Swiss houses today usually have channeled the spring away from their houses or run the spring through culverts. If the farm water source was a well, it would be topped with some device for drawing the water. Some Dutch farms used buckets lowered on cranks to draw water or, more commonly, they used hand pumps. Today, when few people use functioning hand pumps, except some of the Plain people, farms often retain their pumps (or have restored them) as "old-fashioned" ornaments.

Always important was the well-maintained cellar. Cellars were usually dug under only part of the house. A dry, cool basement was important for storing many foods over the winter. If there was a spring, food storage areas would be carefully walled off, away from the water. Most cellar floors were hard packed earth. Characteristically, many German cellars contain large arches that support the massive chimney above. Many food storage areas had plaster directly on the stone walls and were whitewashed to reduce vermin infestation and provide more light.

The physiognomy of the küche has changed over time. Many rooms were retrofitted with cooking stoves in the nineteenth century. As Germans started to emulate their English neighbors, they built end chimney houses with fireplaces or stoves in both the kitchen and the traditional stove room. As the years went on, many families added a new kitchen behind the old küche. The old room was converted into a combination dining room and family room. The old fireplace had often been fitted with doors, which were used in summertime when the great fireplace was not used. This was to keep the birds and animals out. Later the flues were sealed and the old fireplace became a closet. In the twentieth century, many old central chimney stacks were torn out to give the house more floor space suitable for modern living.

Today, old house lovers are delighted to find an intact center chimney—and some have been recreated, as is the case in a house in Cumberland County called "Trout Spring." In truth, though, the kitchens of most Dutch-owned and occupied-traditional homes are as modern as tastes and pocketbooks allow. In interiors you are more likely to find granite counters and stainless steel appliances than you are traditional fireplaces, even among the Plain people.

As soon as they could afford to, many Germans built summer kitchens, separated from the house, where cooking and washing could be done away from the house in warm weather. First built with end-wall fireplaces, many summer kitchens, like the küche, were retrofitted with stoves while later buildings were constructed only for stoves. It is interesting to note that in many households, frugal householders owned only one cook stove. An annual chore was to move the cook stove into the summer kitchen in summer, and back again in the fall. In some areas, stoves were not adopted for many years. The Reverend E.O. Steigerwalt recalled that his grandmother insisted on cooking over an open fire until her death in the 1920s.

Many times, summer houses were fitted with bells, often in a small belfry, which were rung to call workers from the fields for meals. Bells were also sometimes mounted on bell poles near the back door. In most places, the function of the summer kitchen has changed. Some have been attached to the main house by a corridor (some were attached before by an open arcade). Summer kitchens today are utility rooms, family rooms, home offices, or just places to store stuff. On many farms, the summer kitchen has simply been allowed to rot away.

The stube, or stove room, was the most desirable room in the house. When it was heated, it was warm and devoid of smoke and had fewer smells than the kitchen. Not all kitchen odors were desirable—remember the chickens in their cages. The stove room was heated by a five-plate iron stove fed through the back of the kitchen fireplace or by a similarly fired masonry or tile stove. These stoves were especially used by the Moravians who manufactured them in Bethlehem, from the eighteenth century. Reproduction tile stoves continue to be produced today at Moravian workshops in Old Salem in North Carolina. A masonry stove has been recreated at the Hans Herr House in Lancaster

County. Masonry and tile stoves give off an even heat. Many stuben were fitted with built in benches. Those backing onto masonry stoves were especially warm and were favored by the arthritic elderly.

The stube was a multipurpose room. It was a sitting room, but it was also used for home crafts and probably for sleeping as well. In the late eighteenth century, emulating the English, the stube was transformed into a parlor. By the early nineteenth century, this was its usual function. The parlor became a special occasion sitting and receiving room. It is at this time that a second front door is commonly incorporated into the Pennsylvania German house, leading directly into the parlor. This separates the family entrance from the new company entrance and eliminates the need for a center hall.

Separated from the back of the stube is the bedroom, or kammer, which was the most private and remote part of the house. The kammer was never heated. Its function also changed over the years. While in conservative households it might continue as a downstairs bedroom, in others it might become a study or den, as at the Landis House at the Landis Valley Museum. In many instances, as the concept of the multipurpose "living room" replaced the Sunday-only parlor, the wall between the two rooms was removed to create one large room. This was often an easy process because the interior walls of many German houses were simply vertical boards. Similarly, ceilings were generally meant to have open beams. Today, many people associate German interiors with low ceilings, but that is not the case. When ceilings are low, they are later additions added to make the house more fashionable, quieter, and cleaner.

If the house has a second floor, the enclosed staircase that ran along the outside wall, opposite the fireplace, would open into an open rectangular room onto which the chambers, or kammeren opened. Like the chambers below, these rooms lacked heat. The most desirable ones were those through which the chimney stack rose. These were the warmest of the upper-story sleeping rooms.

Many houses like this still exist. When one couple was house hunting in 2003, they were amazed to be shown a house with "gravity heat" on the second floor. The Ruizs were curious. Gravity heat, they reported, consisted of iron grate–protected holes in the floor. "After all," the realtor told them, "heat rises." Here, too, while some older houses are heated with stoves, some traditionally and others because of rising energy costs, most have modern heating systems, often steam or hot water. Central air conditioning is also common. Outdoor condensers are a common sight, or blight, on the landscape.

When indoor plumbing was installed in many of these houses in the early twentieth century, it was common to have the toilet and the tub placed in the hall-room at the head of the stairs. A curtain might provide some privacy. In later years, a bedroom would be sacrificed to a bathroom and to provide closets. Often the space under the stairway on the first floor might be converted into a half bath. One of the most common additions to a traditional house is designed to provide extra bathrooms and closet space, but there is at least one old-house purist whose family would not add closets to any of the bedrooms because they did not want to change the proportion of any rooms. They built closets in their attic instead. They claimed the exercise was good for them, as well as for the architectural integrity of the 1760s house.

Many early houses were one story topped by a high double attic that housed sleeping areas below and grain storage above. On early farms, grain was too valuable to family survival to risk keeping it in the barn, and accordingly it was usually kept in the upper level of the attic.

Under layers of modern siding, many surprises lurk. Half timber, or fachtwerk, houses were known throughout Europe and the British Islands. This perhaps was the construction technique most widely used in our earliest German houses. In half timbering, which is the product of a timber-poor culture, the building is framed with timber. The areas between structural elements are filled in with a variety of materials—often woven branches over lath, sometimes stone, or even brick. Characteristically, the infills are plastered over and left exposed, inside and out. Because of the constant maintenance needed by the plastering, our cold winters, and an abundance of inexpensive wood, most American half-timbered houses were sheathed over many years ago. As fashion changed, most interior walls were also covered over. Half-timbered structures, which are also almost always joined with pegged mortise and tenon joints, are extremely strong, and if foundations settle, they can display amazing flexibility.

THE PENNSYLVANIA DUTCH COUNTRY

The technology was brought into America by subsequent waves of immigrants; not only into Pennsylvania, but into Texas and the Midwest as well. In Pennsylvania, many half-timbered houses were built well into the second half of the nineteenth century. Most that exist today are not recognized for what they are because they are covered by siding. The eighteenth-century Plough Tavern in York, Pennsylvania, was "discovered" and recognized when an observant antiques dealer noted a strange pattern of nails in the siding that covered the fachtwerk. The kitchen of the author's house is half timbered as well. This was discovered during an attempt to insulate what was assumed to be an ordinary frame house.

Log technology was probably first introduced into America in Pennsylvania by the Swedes, who settled here in the 1640s. Known as the pört, we have come to call the homely structure, so adaptable to the wilderness of North America, the log cabin or log house. The cabins, made of hewn, carefully squared logs laid horizontally, fitted tightly together, with little chinking between them, were tight and warm. However, the Swedish tradition of log construction apparently died out rather quickly in the East, although it was reintroduced by Swedish immigrants into the upper Midwest in the 1840s and forward.

Log construction was reintroduced into Pennsylvania by Palatine Germans coming here in numbers from the 1730s. Their structures reflected the Germanic tradition, as the Swedish structures looked back on their Nordic homeland. The chimney placement, floor plan, and log work were distinctively Germanic. German log technology employs rough hewn logs that often require very substantial chinking and plastering between them. Construction was faster and easier then using the Swedish technique. A log—and they were always worked green—could be shaped by a skilled worker using a broad axe in about 30 minutes. It was this German cabin adopted by the English and the Scots Irish, and in some measure adapted by them, which has been imbued with the holy mystic of "log cabinism."

One of the greatest of American myths is that every man could build his own cabin to house his family. Research has proven that this is not true. Every settlement had someone more adept than others at log craft. He often traded his skills for produce and other goods or services.

Log houses were usually chinked with wooden wedges, stones, moss, clay, or a combination of materials. The chinking, in turn, was usually covered with a plaster made of mud, lime, straw, and cow manure. Once a house was built, it was traditionally up to the housewife to keep the plastering intact. A regular autumn project was plaster maintenance. In early homes, the interior of log walls were simply whitewashed. As fashions changed and the Dutch became richer, most log buildings were sheathed. Early on, log houses were covered with wooden siding. In later years, asphalt shingles and even aluminum siding was used. Similarly, interiors were updated with modern wall treatments. Today, literally thousands of log buildings stand, disguised. It should also be noted that some log buildings were built to be covered immediately. Why? Because sheathed log buildings are warm and tight.

In recent years there has been a log revival. Many traditional log buildings have been freed of their sheathing, sometimes with disastrous results. Most modern people do not want to be bothered with traditional plaster so they use tinted cement, which expands at a different coefficient of expansion than do logs and allows water to be trapped, which encourages rotting of the wood. The modern penchant for building contemporary log homes is more related to some frontier mystique than to Pennsylvania German influence. Modern log houses are being built in Pennsylvania, often from kits, today far more are constructed in the West. In fashionable enclaves in Wyoming and Montana, $1 million log vacation homes are almost commonplace. Needless to say, modern log construction eliminates chinking altogether. Thus, their technology is more Scandinavian than German.

Germans are a very conservative people who strongly believe in building for the ages. Above all, Germans respect permanence. Accordingly, the most desirable of building materials is stone, which is also the most difficult material with which to work. The two basic forms of stone work are ashlar, or carefully cut stone; and rough shaped, so called "rubble stone." The choice of building techniques reflected both the pocketbook of the builders and the Germanic region from which they came. Builders in some regions used mortar very generously, so much so that walls almost looked plastered. Others fitted the stone together very carefully using minimal mortar. Beginning in the late eighteenth century, the Germans also started building in brick, a form of masonry easier to work than stone. Brick became the dominant material used by builders seeking permanence. Because brick walls have a tendency to spread, iron tie rods were often inserted through the house. Where they emerged, they were fastened with turn buckles. Some of these were plain circular disks, others were stars or elongated "S" shapes.

Germans favored steep gable roofs. More elaborate houses might have gambrel roofs. Three roofing materials were traditionally employed: tile, wood shingle, and thatching. German roof tiles, formed and baked by tile makers, or zieglers, were made of the same red clay used for brick making and the celebrated Pennsylvania German redware pottery. Tiles would be hung in overlapping ranks on horizontal support elements called purlins. Roof construction had to be especially sturdy to support the heavy tiles. These weight bearing structures could also easily support slate roofs, which became especially popular in the late nineteenth century with the development of the slate industry in Lehigh County. Several original tile roofs survive on houses and outbuildings in Lancaster and Berks Counties.

German-style thatching differs significantly from the more familiar British Islands form where lengths of reeds are laboriously sewn together before being incorporated into the roof. Germans used rye straw tied with the same rye straw into small bundles called fackles. These, in turn, are tied onto a purlin roof to create a thick, weather-tight roof. Rye straw, a byproduct of grain production, was favored because of its durability and its natural insect repellent qualities. Thatching on homes apparently died out by the mid-nineteenth century; however, thatching for agricultural structures continued into the early twentieth century.

Wooden shingles were the most widely used roofing material. German shingles began as shakes, 18 to 24 inches long, split from log sections (often oak), and then tapered into shingles on a shaver's bench, *ein schniztlebank*, with a draw knife. Shingles would be overlapped side-by-side with a single nail holding each in place. Because of the length of the shingle, in fact, each nail penetrated and secured several shingles.

Each of the traditional roofing materials had inherent problems. Tile could absorb water, which could freeze and cause the clay to spall. Tile was, of course, both heavy and increasingly expensive—a fate that would also befall slate. It is interesting to note that there are now both tile and slate revivals in high-end new home construction, which has brought new suppliers into the field and made it possible to find materials more easily for the restoration of historic structures. Additionally, simulations of both tile and slate are widely available, including a very convincing line of aluminum tile.

Thatch was the most fragile of roofing materials and also the most susceptible to fire. Except at museums, there is no call in America for this roofing material. Unlike in Europe, where there is a mystique to thatch and an availability of a plastic version to create the historical illusion, thatch has vanished from our cultural-historical landscape. Wood shingles applied in the traditional manner have similarly disappeared because of the expense of the material and its fire hazard. A properly installed traditional shingle roof will often allow daylight in, but it does not allow rain in as it swells shut; however, snow can blow in. Descriptions of loft sleepers who woke up covered in snow are common. Today, there is an increasing popularity in the use of wood shingles that are treated with a fire retardant and installed in the more familiar Anglo-American tradition.

About the 1840s, standing tin roofs became very popular in German regions. These durable, and once inexpensive, metal roofs replaced many shingle, thatched, and tile roofs and were the roofing of choice for much new construction. Many of the early roof installers were tinsmiths whose traditional craft, the making of household utensils, was threatened with the widespread availability of factory made goods. Metal roofs, in turn, yielded to the cheaper still asphalt roof tiles. Interestingly, there is also a revival in the use of the painted standing tin roofs of yesterday. While they cost more to install than asphalt or fiberglass shingles, they are ultimately more durable and some people like the old-fashioned sound of raindrops on a tin roof.

Every traditional German house, like its Anglo counterparts, had a privy, or outhouse. In rural areas, these survived well into the second half of the twentieth century and are still used on occasional farms. Many other outhouses are used as tool sheds. The Pennsylvania Germans are reticent about sexual jokes, but an inordinate number of their jokes are scatological and especially outhouse centered. "Roadside America," a pioneer Pennsylvania German tourist attraction near Shartlesville, features a miniature train rolling through Dutch countryside. Among other details, spectators can see into an outhouse with a miniature Dutchman sitting on the board.

Early non-German travelers through areas of German settlement seldom commented on the houses or outhouses of the regions, but they were lyrical about the fertility of the soil and the magnificent barns that dwarfed dwellings. The Germans were among the first farmers to appreciate the value of regularly manuring their fields. To collect manure, you had to contain your cattle for a good part of the day, and so barns with animal byres became important. Manure was traditionally collected and piled between the house and the barn. German culture held: "A fat wife and a big manure pile show a man's rich." Ripening manure might also be banked against the north (and often windowless) wall of traditional stone or brick houses. The exothermic reaction of the decomposing manure would heat the cold northern wall of masonry houses.

While many early barns were simply ground barns, i.e., one story and loft buildings where a central thrashing floor separated animal stalls and hay storage, the great classic Pennsylvania German barn is the bank barn. This is a two story and loft barn ideally built into a hillside, but often with the second level accessed by a ramp. The lower level contains the animal byre. The forebay of the upper level of the barn protects the farmer as he tends to his animals. The area under the south-facing forebay effectively catches low rays of the winter sun and keeps the area noticeably warmer than elsewhere in the enclosed barnyard.

While there are antecedents of the bank barn in the British Islands as well as in many parts of Europe, in America the barn form is usually found only in areas of German influence. While there are many variations of the German barn, all of which are completely studied in Robert F. Ensminger's *The Pennsylvania Barn: Its Origin, Evolution, and Destruction in North America* (1992), there are two basic forms of the barn. The most spectacular is often the "Sweitzer" or "Swiss" version, which has a cantilevered forebay. The "German" or "Dutch" barn has a supported forebay. Often the supports can be very aesthetically pleasing. Additionally enhancing the beauty of a barn are ventilators. It is very important that grain and hay storage areas be well ventilated. Dust suspended in stagnant air can be explosive. The simplest ventilators are often simply slits. Nineteenth-century myth makers often said these were gun slits to protect against Native American raids. Later barns often have window-size louvered openings and louvered cupolas on the roof as well.

Barns are built of log, frame, or masonry. Prosperous multi-generational farms often have an early ground barn, or grundscheier, now used for storage, and a working bank barn. Log barns were most likely to have been thatched into the twentieth century. Framed barns continue the tradition of mortise, tenon, and peg construction of fachtwerk, or half timbering, but they are not infilled, simply sheathed. Because fire is an ever-present danger because of spontaneous combustion, dust explosions, or lightning strikes, many masonry barns are built with sturdy supporting walls. The remainder of the barn is of easier to replace materials. Early barns were usually small because they only had to house the few animals used for subsistence farming. With the post-railroad rise of commercial dairying, barns became ever larger and grander. The barn was truly the Pennsylvania German farmer's cathedral. Garrison Kiellor, creator of PBS's popular *A Prairie Home Companion* radio show, recalls that when a boy in a Lutheran family (of Norwegian background) heard the term "Lutheran Bishop," he would always imagine the leader to be the one who had the largest barn!

One of the Dutch country's best-known and most-loved barns is the landmark "Star Barn" in Dauphin County, which is in sight of a super highway, Route 283, near Middletown. Built by William Motter (1822–1901) in the 1870s, it is clearly a gentleman's barn. It was originally surrounded by a wide range of farm buildings, some of which remain, whose weathervanes, now gone, expressed each structure's use. The barn's great louvered gable-end stars and its Gothic lath-filled "windows" are ventilators designed to ensure that dust never built up into combustible levels in the "Cathedral of Barns." Saved from decay by the Millport Foundation, a local organization with Dutch roots, its future use is uncertain.

Barn functions have changed. As dairy farming has become more important, silos were added, beginning in the 1850s, to store silage and grain for animal feed. The large familiar metal silos are a twentieth-century addition to the landscape. On most active farms today, the barns are used mostly for storage. Modern dairying techniques demand different milking arrangements than those for which German barns were designed. Modern farm equipment is often too large and too heavy to be stored in barns. Very often today, metal sheds have replaced traditional barns in function. Modern hay storage leaves huge plastic-clad rolls in the fields where animals will feed, obviating the need for barn space.

Barns, with their large wooden surfaces in continual need of paint, are expensive to maintain. They have been described as "America's vanishing landmark." Many barns have simply decayed, others have been demolished for their lumber, while some have been carefully dismantled and moved to other parts of the country to be re-assembled. Still others have been the victims of arson. Barn fires are spectacular and have often been set by arsonists—often thrill seekers.

The landscape is dotted with barns that have been adapted to other uses. The most fortunate are maintained on gentlemen's farms, often housing a few horses. Some have been turned into homes, like one visible from Route 441 in Bainbridge in Lancaster County. Others serve as garages on "farmettes," a term real estate folks have coined to describe a cluster of farm buildings that remain on a small plot of land after most of the farm acreage has been sold. Others serve as artist studios or are even used to house indoor swimming pools. The saddest ones generally are those that have been unsympathetically adapted to commercial use. Although there are exceptions—a barn near Mount Joy has been turned into offices so sensitively that you hardly notice the transition—more often, barns are converted into furniture stores or, especially on tourist routes, "Dutch gift shoppes."

Every farm community needed its grist mill, used to convert grain into flour. Often built of stone, many of these early water-powered mills were adapted to steam and later diesel power, and many operated early into the twentieth century. A few limped on even longer. Some are run as tourist attractions today. Many are derelict; others have been converted into antiques shops or homes. They remain a common sight in rural Dutch country.

Dutchland towns are distinctive. The smaller communities tend to be linear, often one street deep, with the houses built right up to the property (now the sidewalk line) with no front yards. In many towns, like Stouchsburg in Berks

County, the deep backyards end in small barns used for keeping a cow or two for family use. Backyards certainly housed chickens, perhaps a pig or two, and caged rabbits, as well as a vegetable garden. German-settled towns tend to end in "burg" as in Strasburg, or the even more Germanic "dorf," as in Wormelsdorf. Towns settled by British Island folks often end in "ville," like Wellsville, but many of these soon had predominantly Germanic populations, as well.

Of the cities in the region, Lancaster perhaps retains the most German architecture, although York and Reading also have some Germanic structures. But most surviving buildings are more reflective of wider community tastes. This shift to the architectural values of the Anglo world is visible in the details of many older houses, but it is more dramatic in public buildings. For example, the structure that now serves as the Heritage Center Museum of Lancaster County is a mixture of Georgian and Federal styles. Located on Penn Square, in the center of Lancaster City, it was built between 1795 and 1798 as the Public Offices to serve the nearby second Lancaster County Courthouse, which stood in the center of Penn Square until it was razed in 1853. When the present courthouse was finished, the building was considered redundant and it was sold to Lancaster City, which used it as its City Hall until 1932. English in form and clearly reflecting the influence of Philadelphia, the building represents the collaborative effort of German artisans John Lind (1761–1823), and his lesser-known contemporaries Jacob Flubacher and Joshua W. Jack.

Also part of the present Heritage Center complex is the Federal style Masonic Lodge Hall and market spaces built between 1795 and 1798 by Lancaster joiner Gottlieb Sehner (Sener, Soehner). The building's magnificent assembly hall was restored in the 1930s by Lancaster City's first homegrown resident architect Cassius Emlen Urban, whose family and given names demonstrate the acculturation of an aspiring German family. Urban's great-grandfather Ludwig was a well-to-do Conestoga Township farmer at the time of the Revolution. Born in Conestoga Township, Urban's father Amos S. (1838–1888), moved to Lancaster City and became prosperous as a partner in a planing mill, a building supplies dealer, and a sometimes speculative builder. Grandiloquently named, Cassius Emlen was born in 1863. After graduating from Lancaster Boy's High School, he studied architecture by working in offices in Scranton and Philadelphia, most notably as a draftsman for the well-known Philadelphia architect Willis G. Hale (1848–1907). Returning to his native city in the 1880s, Urban designed many of the most important buildings in the city, including its only skyscraper, the Greist Building, before his death in 1939.

Very Germanic, and still surviving in the cities and countryside of the region, are the market areas, sometimes called market squares, occupied first by open market stalls, then by market houses. Today, Harrisburg, Lancaster, and York house flourishing market houses, sometimes called "Farmer's Markets" by outsiders. Locals call them simply "Market," except in places like Lancaster, which had several market houses into the twentieth century. Only "Central Market" survives. Historically, markets were held on Tuesday and Friday. Now many have added Saturday hours as well. In the countryside, there are sprawling rural "Farmer's Markets," including the Green Dragon and Roots, both in Lancaster County. Both are twentieth century in origin, and both on their days of operations (Roots, for example, is only open on Tuesday) are wonderful places to see Plain people, church people, and every other type of person intermingle in a fair-like atmosphere.

Chapter Three

DUTCH GARDENS AND FOODWAYS

Food and Pennsylvania Dutch go together well, like ham and eggs or ice cream and apple pie. The bounty of Pennsylvania Dutch farms and gardens shows up in the plenty of the traditional table. Just as German farms had a distinctive look, so too did their gardens; be they in the country or behind houses in town. The oldest surviving garden plans that relate to the evolution of the Pennsylvania German kitchen garden are the medicinal gardens of the Benedictine cloisters of Saint Gall in Switzerland and Reichenau in Germany. Plans dating from the 1600s for their berbularis, or herb gardens, called for "creating a quadrant innenbof [courtyard] or atrioluse [small atrium] and dividing it into garden beds." In turn, this plan was copied and adopted in cloisters and monasteries throughout Europe. By the Middle Ages, the enclosed kitchen garden, laid out in quadrants with raised beds and pathways between them, was widely promoted as the most efficient way of providing the vegetable needs for a household. By the Renaissance, city views show that this type of garden was widely used in urban settings as well. It was this tried-and-true garden form that immigrants from what now constitutes modern Germany and Switzerland brought with them to Pennsylvania.

To this day, many Pennsylvania Germans retain a closeness to the soil that goes beyond mere occupation. It has religious overtones. "Perhaps it has something to do with their unique history, perhaps it has something to do with their sense of clan and place," speculates scholar John Frantz, a longtime faculty member, now retired from the Pennsylvania State University and an authority on Pennsylvania German history. Frantz is an avid gardener who professes that he "can't help himself" when spring comes. His garden has strong traditional overtones.

In addition to a passion for gardening, the Pennsylvania Germans maintain a strong desire to preserve ancestral seeds, perhaps summed up in the saying,

THE PENNSYLVANIA DUTCH COUNTRY

Gude Sume, Gude Gaarde (good seeds, good garden). An extraordinary number of American heirloom seed varieties bear the prefix "German" or "Amish."

In sharp distinction to the general American concept of vegetable gardening as a male pursuit, the Pennsylvania German kitchen garden was always considered to be primarily the woman's province. The men in the family were expected to build the garden, spread manure on the beds in fall, and turn over the soil for spring planting, but the women and children planted, weeded, watered, and harvested. The most common Pennsylvania Dutch garden contained four symmetrical raised garden beds, although six, eight, or other even numbers of beds were not unknown. The beds were divided by narrow paths of packed earth, and the gardeners' regular attention to the beds was all that was required to keep weeds in the paths to a minimum. Paving was rare. The raised beds were usually bordered with planks of first-growth pine or oak (good woods that would last for 20 to 30 years, much longer than modern-day lumber), which was held in place by stakes of the same wood 8 to 12 inches high.

The garden was always fenced, historically with a pale or picket fence, which was inexpensive in an age of abundant first-growth lumber—long lasting, and most important of all, allowed for a free flow of air in the garden, very necessary in the humid summers of Eastern and South Central Pennsylvania. The principal function of the fence was to keep animals out, particularly rabbits, but also skunks, raccoons, and groundhogs—all notorious crop destroyers. Deer, the bane of modern gardeners, were no problem for the Pennsylvania Germans, who simply slaughtered them for meat whenever they could. The author's 90-year-old mother-in-law, who grew up on a traditional Dutch farm that included a fruit orchard, reveals that she never saw a wild deer until she was in her twenties. Garden fences, therefore, did not have to be excessively high. The fence, in most cases, was between 36 and 40 inches high, and the pales typically extended into the ground or into a sill board that extended into the ground. Additionally, the pales were close together, seldom more than several inches apart, and the top of each one was cut into a point, symmetrically or on a diagonal, which allowed rainwater to drain easily, preventing the wood from rotting, and also made the fence uncomfortable to scale and unpleasant for a marauding cow to graze over. Pales were attached by two nails—one near the top, one near the bottom—to the supporting rails, and the nails were reused when the fence needed to be replaced.

The prime function of the raised beds was to promote easy drainage, but they also allowed for conditioning the soil so that the gardener could grow a larger assortment of crops than would be successful otherwise. Because of the quick drainage of the beds, cool-soil vegetables like English (sweet) peas, lettuces, spring onions, and radishes could be planted earlier than they could in the surrounding fields, where wet conditions would rot the precious seeds. If the soil on the farm or homestead was heavy clay, or rocky, one or more beds might be filled with sieved soil, enhanced with sand, so that root crops like carrots could grow to their full potential. Great attention was paid to keeping the soil in beds friable and loose. Cultivation was never done with a plow or a cultivator, but always with a hoe. When planting rows, boards were often placed across the edging planks so that the gardener could lean into the bed without having to rest the weight of her hand on the soil.

What was grown in the kitchen garden varied with time, but it is important to note that a differentiation was made between field and garden crops. Staples, such as cabbages, potatoes, turnips, and field peas, were usually grown in the fields. Generally the kitchen garden provided at least two crops per bed per year. Besides those already mentioned, favored garden plantings included peppers, eggplant, tomatoes, cucumbers, and melons. Spinach and fancy cabbages like crinkled-leaf savoy were also popular, as were specialty corns, such as popping corn.

Many foursquare gardens were bordered with additional beds that followed the perimeter fencing. The fences could then be used to support vines or brambles. Cucumber vines might be trained on the fence, along with hopvines, the dried flowers of which were used in making bread and beer, as well as a pillow filling that was highly regarded as a soporific for insomniacs. These border beds might also be used for small fruits like currants or raspberries, or for medicinal or flavoring herbs.

While the layout of the traditional Pennsylvania Dutch garden is derived from the herb gardens of monasteries, the Dutch did not have herb gardens as we understand them. These were a creation of the colonial revival of the late nineteenth and early twentieth centuries. Traditional German cookery used few flavor enhancers besides salt and pepper (if available). The most commonly grown seasonings were onions, parsley, sage, and dill, which was highly favored for pickling. Saffron, the product of Crocus savitus, an autumn-blooming flower that is notoriously laborious to harvest, was also very commonly cultivated, although today it is grown by few gardeners, most of whom are Mennonites. The other highly favored condiment plant, horseradish, was rarely if ever grown in a garden because of its invasive nature. The same is true of members of the mint family, which the Germans brewed into teas and gave great medicinal credit to as well. The rare Pennsylvania Dutch Roman Catholic sometimes placed a potted rosemary in the center of a foursquare garden, but its significance was religious— associated with the Virgin Mary—not culinary. Along these lines, Pennsylvania Dutch Protestants often planted an Adam and Eve plant (Yucca filamentosa) in the middle of their gardens. However, how this American native plant came to be considered an expression of Protestant faith is not known.

Traditionally, the Pennsylvania Dutch garden was placed on level ground, although the archaeologically correct, recreated garden at Burnside Plantation, a Moravian site in Bethlehem, Pennsylvania, is on a terraced slope. Most important was the availability of water, for raised gardens drained so well that they needed to be watered more frequently than flat gardens. Pennsylvania German farms were invariably laid out on an east-west axis, with the house and barn facing south (as noted earlier) and the garden usually placed near the kitchen door, where it could share a water source, generally a well or spring, with the house. A garden needs at least 1 inch of water per week, so the chore could be arduous indeed in times of drought, when it might be necessary to fill and haul buckets from more distant water sources. Watering cans were considered a luxury until inexpensive machine-made galvanized-metal ones became available about 1900.

The Pennsylvania Dutch were among the first farmers to barn, pen, and pasture their animals, practices that allowed them to collect manure, which they applied liberally to both gardens and fields. They did not use compost, but often placed their garden near the pigpen, chicken yard, or rabbit hutches so that these animals could convert less palatable garden produce into manure.

Among the most dedicated of gardeners, different manures were, and are, preferred for particular crops.

Flowers, per se, had no place in Pennsylvania Dutch kitchen gardens, although some plants we consider ornamental were grown for their food value. Nasturtiums, for instance, were often raised for their buds, which were pickled to provide a caper substitute; the tender leaves of calendulas, or "Pot Marigolds" (Calendula officinalis) were eaten as a vegetable and the flowers were used as a dyestuff. Occasionally, French marigolds (Tagetas patula), which the Germans called, in translation, "stinky flowers," were grown among beans to repel beetles. In this vein, it is important to remember that although the Pennsylvania Dutch had to contend with fewer garden pests than we do today, the problem has always existed. They occasionally used lethal, but organic, substances such as tobacco dust and arsenic-based compounds to deter insects, but a good deal of pest control was purely mechanical: the women and children hand picked insects, snails, and slugs. This is still the most effective organic method of pest control.

The traditional Pennsylvania Dutch garden was eventually abandoned because of increasing interaction with the English world and the rising importance of commercial seed houses and commercial or truck farming. The final blow was the widespread availability of the rototiller after World War II. When power machinery entered the picture, vegetable gardening among nonsectarian Pennsylvania Dutch appears to have shifted to men.

In the past two decades, there has been a revival of appreciation for the raised-bed garden, both by organic gardeners and by historic sites and museums. Organic gardeners appreciate the virtues of a garden that allows for the use of compost rather than chemical fertilizer and a form that provides substantial yields in a small area. Among the most influential historical sites that have carefully revived the traditional German garden is the Landis Valley Museum near Lancaster, which not only has a very fine period garden, but is also home to the Heirloom Seed Project, which makes traditional Pennsylvania Dutch varieties of vegetable and flower seeds widely available.

Pennsylvania Dutch food is not diet cuisine by any modern standard, Dr. Atkins included. It is a meat and potato and noodle cooking diet where vegetables are never served without additional calories, usually animal fat and/or sugar. But as traditional cookery expert William Woys Weaver points out in his *Pennsylvania Dutch Country Cooking*, Dutch food has changed a great deal from the eighteenth century: "Yet above all else," Weaver observes, "it is a cookery with a sense of place, a cuisine that recognizes the unchanging essence of Bodegeschmach, meaning that our food has in it the taste of the land."

Central to traditional German baking and cooking was the grain spelt (Triticum spelta), which has almost entirely disappeared from our cooking. Germans grew wheat for the marketplace and employed its flour for special occasions, but usually they used spelt, which yielded grain as prolifically as oats. Spelt, which the Dutch call Dinkel, has a high gluten content, and even today in Germany spelt is the only flour used to make gingerbread. Weaver observes:

> Spelt was used in Pennsylvania Dutch cookery as a form of grits, as a whole grain cooked like rice, as a whole grain harvested green and smoked for use in soups, as a meal in porridges, and as a flour in breads, pastries, and dumplings. Spelt and barley meal were used to make square-shaped johnny cakes that were wrapped in cabbage leaves and baked on hot coals. Spelt and barley flour, mixed with saffron and honey, are still the primary ingredients of the Christmas gingerbread men made in the New Berlin area of Union County.

In Weaver's book, one discovers recipes that most living, traditional Dutch folk would find unfamiliar, including "Spelt Soup with Hickory Nut Dumplings" (*Dinkelsupp Mit Hickerniss-Gnepp*); Schales, a shallow dish casserole; and "Smoked Eel Soup with Hominy" (*G'Schmokte-Ohlesupp Mit Hahmini*). His recipe for chickweed pie is also very unfamiliar, but a sensible way to deal with a spring weed among a people famous for wasting nothing. In true Dutch fashion, the pie derives its real flavor from smoked bacon—a Dutch favorite.

Along with various familiar noodle recipes, Weaver also gives a definitive recipe for one of the more complex Dutch dishes, "Stuffed Pigs Stomach" or "Dutch Goose." *Dietcher* [sic] *Gans* is a pig stomach stuffed with a mixture of onions, sausage, potatoes, breadcrumbs, and herbs. After baking, it is served sliced. When the author's father-in-law was ailing, he could always be tempted to eat with a portion of pig stomach acquired from a nearby restaurant, The Country Table in Mount Joy, where it was an every-Wednesday special.

Dutch food was changed slowly from its European antecedents by thousands of housewives cooking over the centuries. What affected the cuisine greatly was the widespread availability of refined sugar and canned lard in the post–Civil War years. These allowed for foods to be made sweeter—and the famous "seven sweets and seven sours" emerged as accompaniments to meat dishes. Lard could now be used year-round for baking where, in earlier years, it was used mostly around harvest time and finished off before Lent with the making of Fastnacht, the fried donuts traditionally served on Shrove Tuesday using up the year's lard. It is a powerful cultural statement to compare the fact that the French in America celebrate Fat Tuesday, Mardi Gras, with an orgy of riotous celebration. The Dutch eat fried dough and let it go at that. J. George Frederick notes that Fastnacht Day "once included a fasting period at some obscure ancient time, but the Dutch never fast!" Traditional fastnachts are square and incised with a cross. Originally, they were eaten unembellished, after their "swim in hot fat," or dunked in molasses or coffee. Most are now sold sprinkled with sugar or even glazed. Numerous churches in Dutch country make fastnachts as a money maker—but on Shrove Tuesday, every supermarket in Dutch country sells some semblance of them.

Another holiday-associated pastry treat are the various kinds of cookies—all sweet—many fashioned with fanciful cookie cutters in animal, human, or flower shapes. Dutch families often had a dozen or more cutters amassed over the years. Shaped cookies were especially popular at Christmas. Folklorist Alfred Shoemaker remembers "the Pennsylvania-German cookie baking and eating that occurred in the valleys of the Lehigh, the Schuylkill, and the Susquehanna [were] a veritable orgy." Cookies were strung for decorations and eaten all through December. Moravian Sugar Cake was traditionally served on Christmas Eve as well as after regular Sunday evening services. "The oldest and most traditional shape for the cake was round, the same size as the wooden peels on which they were raised."

Pies have a very special place in Dutch cookery and they were made in an amazing variety. Not only a desert food, pie, often in two or three kinds, was considered a good breakfast food to supplement ham and eggs and cooked cereal. The pie at breakfast went out of vogue as farmers left the land and fewer calories were needed. Cookbook author and restaurant owner Betty Groff recalled that she always served pie at breakfast while her husband Abe farmed. She kept it up awhile after he turned to managing their business interests, "but then he started to blow up." Pies soon left the Groff breakfast table.

Fruit pies were especially popular, made in season from the expected cherries, grapes, blueberries, raspberries, blackberries, or apples. Among the more unusual fruit pies are green tomato, groundberry (husk tomato), and green currant pie. In winter, fruit pies were made from dried apples or schnitz, dried cherries, or raisins. Raisin or dried cherry pies were often called "funeral pies" because they were traditionally served at funeral meals—being the best pie stuffs available in winter. Intimately related to Dutch culture is the molasses-based Shoofly pie, which is at least nineteenth century in origin. It is available in many variants—wet bottom, dry bottom, and even chocolate flavored. Many other pies, like chickweed pie, were meant for lunch and dinner as the main dish or as an accompaniment to meats. These included parsley pie, potato custard pie, chicken cornmeal pie, cabbage pork pie, and corn pie. Chicken-pot-pie is one of the most famous Dutch dishes, but it is really a cross between a casserole and a thick soup. Made without a crust, pot pie is made of homemade egg noodles, potatoes, chicken meat, onions, and celery, and is best when redolent with saffron.

The Dutch have been called the "Sauerkraut Yankees" because of their love of the fermented cabbage, which was a winter staple in their diet. For good luck all year, you must eat pork and sauerkraut on New Year's Day, but pork and sauerkraut is also the quintessential comfort food of even the most casually culture-oriented Dutch and is regularly found on restaurant menus. It is served either on mashed potatoes or with boiled potatoes and a rich gravy made from the pan drippings when the pork was roasted. Many local volunteer fire companies serve pork and sauerkraut dinners on New Year's Day as a fund raiser. Green beans, ham, and potatoes are also very popular.

The green beans, either fresh or dried, are simmered with the smoked meat for hours until everything is extremely tender. A little cider vinegar is the favored condiment when the meal is eaten. *Schnitz un Gnepp* is another signature dish. It combines smoked pork, dried apples, and dumplings (*Gnepp*).

Pork has always been the preferred meat among the Dutch. Traditionally, fresh pork was only available at butchering time, in November and December. The rest of the year, preserved pork, usually pickled or smoked (ham and bacon, for example) was eaten. The Dutch were proud to claim that when they butchered a pig, "the only thing they didn't use was the squeal." To employ less tender cuts and scraps, they developed a whole range of sausages, puddings, head cheeses (or souse), and scrapple. All are still readily available in the region, many made commercially by Kunzlers, a 100-year-old regional meat packer, and other smaller suppliers. There are still a few, a dwindling number, of craftsmen butchers who smoke their own meats. One is Bob Howry of Willow Street, Lancaster County, whose hams and bacon are a regular part of local larders. Interestingly, the most distinctive local sausage is summer sausage, or Lebanon bologna, which is traditionally made of beef. Heavily and distinctively seasoned, "Lebanon," as it is called, is a "born-with" or, more rarely, an acquired taste.

Fish was never an important part of Dutch diet, but in spring when shad ran in the local rivers, large numbers were caught and eaten fresh. Shad roe was also a Dutch favorite. When the railroad came into Dutch country in the mid-nineteenth century, it made it possible for fresh oysters to be brought up from the Chesapeake Bay in great numbers, and oysters became a regular part of the cuisine of all but the most isolated of the Dutch. Fried oysters and oyster stew were special favorites, and many local churches featured oyster suppers as fund raisers. As oysters have become scarcer and entered the realm of gourmet food, chicken corn soup has replaced them at fund raising events.

As suggested earlier, the Dutch have, since at least the nineteenth century, served sweets and sours with their meals. The mystical "seven" figure is mostly mythology, but the Dutch have a tremendous variety of pickles and preserves, including among the sours green and ripe tomato pickle, pickled cucumbers, pickled Jerusalem artichokes, and most famously, Chow-Chow, which involves lots of vegetables left at the end of harvest season cut in small pieces and preserved in a sweetened brine. Among the sweets are quince honey, rhubarb marmalade, sweet watermelon rind pickle, and apple butter. Apple butter is made by cooking peeled and cored apple slices in cider for many hours with constant stirring to get a thick brown liquid that is often spiced with cinnamon and cloves and often sweetened, today, with extra sugar. Its partner, traditionally, is Schmearkees, a spreading cheese very like cottage cheese, which is often used as a substitute today. Schmearkees and apple butter are spread on thick slices of bread—the flavors complementing one another. Still made frequently is "cup cheese," which is a slightly aged pungent cheese that has the appearance and texture of petroleum jelly. Pierced tin cheese molds, often seen in antique and gift shops, were used to make egg cheese or tsierkase, a rich sweet food popular with the Dutch and considered a traditional Easter food by many.

The best Dutch food is still found in private homes, but today fewer and fewer people cook traditionally, even among the Plain people. Outsiders are always surprised to learn that the Amish eat a lot of prepared snack food. To be close to the soil, and fresh ingredients, does not guarantee a taste preference. Very popular among the Amish are "whoopie pies," a regional pastry consisting of rounds of soft chocolate-flavored cake held together by marshmallow spread. Visitors to the Dutch region are also often surprised to see prayer-veiled Mennonite ladies and fully-garbed Amish eating at local Chinese buffet restaurants.

All of this is a very far distance from the traditional mode of cookery and food preparation recalled by author J. George Frederick (1882–1964), writing about his grandmother in the 1930s, a world with eighteenth-century overtones:

> From the first, my grandmother's genius with food astounded and fascinated me. In her long lifetime of 88 years her hands were never still and no conjurer ever pulled rabbits out of a hat with the facility that she exercised with food from May until December, in preparing and producing an endless variety of things to eat. It is probably literally true that if all the food she produced in her lifetime could be piled in one heap, it would be taller than the

tallest Egyptian pyramid! She produced food of course not only for her family and the farm-hands, but wagon-loads of it to sell each week, winter and summer, in the city farm market-place. Rising at four she would go to the city with grandfather to sell what she had made.

I rarely saw my grandmother buy anything at a grocery store except sugar, salt, pepper, coffee, and a few other things. She usually even made her own baking powder (there is an old Dutch recipe for it), and certainly she never deigned to buy even tea, for she gathered pennyroyal, mint and other herbs in the summer, dried them and they made very good tea indeed.

To fully appreciate my tale of my grandmother's remarkably extensive food skills (which thousands of other Dutch grandmothers of ten generations could equal, and do equal in some Dutch regions even today), you will need to realize several facts.

First of all, you will need to realize that America was developed on this economic principle: the principle of self-sustaining farms, which purchased almost nothing and manufactured almost everything it needed. Thus the colonists created the wealth of America.

Second, you will need to realize that the Pennsylvania Dutch were almost from the very first (unlike most other early American colonists) a farm people; a very versatile and skilled people, and above all a quite exceptionally industrious and thrifty people.

Third, you will need to realize that the Dutch were never content to be only self-sustaining—they brought their section of America up to farming prosperity and fertility faster than the people of any other section in America—by becoming particularly active farm producers and sellers of surplus. The Lancaster County Dutch carried their surplus as much as fifty miles to market over rough colonial trails in their great Conestoga wagons. As nowhere else in America therefore the Dutch developed farm market-places, which are even today unique sights and characteristics of such cities as Philadelphia, Lancaster, Reading, etc. These are street stands where farmers sell from their wagons, or large market buildings where the farmers have stalls.

Fourth, you will need to realize that the Dutch farm housewife was a vital if not dominating part of this plan of farm production and marketing farm surplus. She became a master of a phenomenally wide range of food manufacturing arts; and furthermore she went personally to market in the market-wagons, to meet her customers face-to-face, and to insure that her good products reached the consumer fresh, clean and pure. Thus the Dutch farm family reaped all the profits, both of manufacture, transportation, wholesaling and distribution. That is how they prospered, and prosper today; that indeed is why even the depression has not seriously harmed the Dutch families still engaged in this early colonial farm economics.

In the 1930s, Frederick was already lamenting the passing of regional foods. He believed in:

> a higher standard of taste . . . people who were not born and fed in regions which had special culinary prides and repertoires, virtually never acquire any real food discrimination. They will placidly eat "railroad station pie" or drink "coffee shop slop" all their lives without rebellion; scarcely knowing that they are entitled to something better. Their palates have been ruined during the impressionable period of youth, and food never matters much to them thereafter, except as necessary nourishment.

Frederick realized that until a few years ago, "there were several famous Dutch gourmet paradises, especially near Reading." He especially fondly remembered Kuechler's Roost on Mount Penn, which had "acquired fame in half a dozen states." No provincial, Frederick lamented that in Philadelphia, Lancaster, and Allentown, "similar misfortunes overtook old gourmet retreats; but even famous old restaurants in Paris are meeting the same fate."

While Dutch food available in restaurants has changed over the years, it has not disappeared and, indeed, in the last few years there has been a revival of sorts. However, the traditional Dutchman serving up fantastic traditional food in unpretentious surroundings has certainly disappeared. In the late 1960s, Glen Wolfe served a procession of seasonal Dutch food including spring lettuce with cream dressing and stuffed beef heart in the Colonial Inn in Middletown, Dauphin County, an unrestored early nineteenth-century inn. After Wolfe's death, the eatery went through many hands. Today, it is called Guido McNeals, and the food served is decidedly mainstream.

The beginnings of capitalizing on Pennsylvania Dutch foods among tourists can perhaps be traced to the Shartlesville Inn in Berks County where, in the 1930s, an enterprising innkeeper started featuring "Family Meals, with Seven Sweets and Seven Sours" in a Victorian-era building on old Route 22 between New York and the Dutch country. The restaurant achieved national fame with a *Saturday Evening Post* article in the 1940s. The Shartlesville Inn, outside the developing Pennsylvania Dutch tourist areas of Lancaster County, limped along into the 1990s. Down the street, Haags Hotel still carries on the tradition.

After World War II, several large Dutch home-style restaurants were built and continue to thrive, serving an ersatz version of traditional foods to thousands of Lancaster County tourists each week. The first of these was the Plain and Fancy. It was soon followed by Good and Plenty. All feature lots of food served family style with a limited menu of popular favorites. Perhaps the best Dutch food available in a restaurant today is at Groff's Farm in Mount Joy, Lancaster County, where much of the food is traditional, rich, and wonderful. Perhaps the best compliment the restaurant got was from the Reverend E.O. Steigerwalt, who was taken there for a meal. He enjoyed the food, but remarked, "What's all the fuss about this place? It's just good food."

A food company based in Cumberland County sells "Pennsylvania Dutch" branded snacks and specialty items all up and down the east coast. Somehow, Chow-Chow does not seem right in Rockport, Maine. Real Pennsylvania Dutch food, like the culture, belongs in the region where it developed—and still thrives.

Chapter Four

"PENNSYLVANIA DUTCH STUFF"

Riding through the Dutch countryside, you have to become aware of hex signs first. You may see them in their natural habitat on barns, but you will more probably see them in souvenir shops, or even decorating the placemats in the restaurant where you stop for lunch.

Like agricultural peoples everywhere, the Dutch have their superstitions. They traditionally believed in magical amulets and symbols whose origins often predate their deeply held Christianity. Some of these are repellent to modern tastes and sensibility—for example, nailing the external genitalia of a slaughtered cow to a barn door, and/or the tails of marauders like foxes and raccoons. Prayers written on small pieces of paper were often placed in the joints of timbers. Usually to keep witches away, askew crosses were scratched into the lintels above the entrance to animal stalls. These are almost invisible except to the knowing eye—physical or spiritual. Symbolism and magic go hand-in-hand. The full story of this phenomenon is found in a book by one of the premier scholars of Dutch culture, Don Yoder. In *Pennsylvania Dutch Barn Symbols and Their Meanings*, Yoder concludes that while some endowed the showy hex signs with magic qualities, mostly they are "just for pretty." Yet one Dutch scholar observed that, "even folks who didn't believe in them felt safer with them on the barn." That said, in the days before tourism, hex signs were not found on barns throughout Dutch country, mostly just in parts of Berks, Northampton, and Montgomery Counties.

Under the leadership of several craftsmen, most notably Johnny Ott, whose student Eric Claypoole and the latter's son, Johnny, continue his work, there has been a "hex sign revival," or perhaps an adaptation. Highly decorative hex signs, whose meaning, if any, is still highly disputed, probably first appeared on barns in the Berks County area around 1850 at the time when these structures started to be painted. While some revivalists still paint barn decorations (traditionally the hex signs are repainted when the barn is so old hex signs are virtually non-existent), the bulk of their income is derived from painting (or silk screening) plaques designed to be mounted, depending on size and materials, on your kitchen or den wall or on your garage or storage shed. The new hex signs appeal to Dutch sentimentalists, and even more to tourists. To enhance tourist income, Johnny Ott even devised a shamrock hex sign that is now a Claypoole best seller. Eric Claypoole can be seen decorating a barn and Johnny painting his hex plaques in the videotape *Expressions of Common Hands*, which is also a fine visual introduction to several traditional German crafts.

Jacob Zook (1915–2000), "The Hex Man of Paradise," who worked in the very un-Eden-like town of Paradise in Lancaster County, was another famed hex artist who had an active business along Lancaster's Route 30 tourist corridor. Known for his original designs, he even created (to great national publicity) a custom hex sign for then President Dwight David Eisenhower, himself proudly of Pennsylvania German ancestry. Eisenhower remains a common Dutch belt name.

Commerce has adopted the hex sign imagery, using it on a range of inappropriate or even ludicrous tourist souvenirs ranging from pencils, key chains, and glasses to cocktail napkins and ashtrays.

Working in both watercolor and oil, there have always been folk artists and memorists who have sought to create works of art to glorify their religion, to embellish their homes, or to record their world or that of their neighbors. John Landis (1805–1851) specialized in religious paintings often based on biblical prints. Amish folk artists Henry Lapp (1862–1904) and Barbara Ebersole's (1846–1922) small pictures have a great deal of charm and a breath of innocence. Jacob Maentel's (or Maentle's) many paintings of his contemporaries in Pennsylvania and Indiana are a window into the past. Maentle (1763–1863) was born in Cassel in Germany where he studied medicine. More cosmopolitan than most artists of his ilk, he is said to have been one of Napoleon's secretaries. Coming to America he eventually joined the Economie Society at New Harmony, Indiana. The society, founded by George Rapp, a Swabian from the principality of Würtenberg, created three communities: Harmony in Pennsylvania, New Harmony in Indiana, and finally Economy in Beaver County, Pennsylvania.

"Pennsylvania Dutch Stuff"

Lewis Miller (1795–1882) was born of German immigrants in York County. A carpenter and amateur artist, Miller's illuminated diaries and memoirs are as close as one can get in America to incunabula adventures. In their pages you meet many citizens of York, Pennsylvania—both fine and venal, and you see what is among the earliest illustrations of a Christmas tree in American art. Like Maentel, Lewis Miller was more cosmopolitan than he would seem. He traveled to Baltimore, New York City—and even to Europe. His books are treasured at the York County Historical Society and the Abby Aldrich Rockefeller Folk Art Museum.

Ferdinand A. Brader (1833–1890s) was an itinerant artist about whose life almost nothing is known. He did his most extensive works in the Berks County countryside where, on commission, he drew detailed pencil drawings of local farms. These works are invaluable to students of Pennsylvania German farms, architecture, and gardening. Executed on ordinary brown paper, many of the drawings are quite large: 30x30 inches is not uncommon. A master letterer, Brader's delineations are usually captioned with the name of the property, the township, and the county. Later in life, probably seeking more work in an age of rising competition, he moved west across Pennsylvania and into Ohio.

Hattie Brunner (1889–1982) has been described as "the Pennsylvania German Grandma Moses." Like Anna Mary Robertson Moses (1860–1961), Hattie came to painting late in life. In common with much about the Pennsylvania Germans, this genial lady from Reinholds, in Berks County, who spoke with a thick Dutch accent, was not as transparent as she would appear. She was a shrewd businesswoman who had been one of the first antiques dealers to develop a market for Pennsylvania German materials. She became the principal supplier of Dutch antiques for Henry Francis du Pont and items acquired from her are the heart of the Winterthur Museum's extensive Pennsylvania German collection. Only when the supply of extraordinary antiques began to dry up did she start to paint in earnest. Brunner's work today is highly valued; while in her lifetime she seldom sold any work for $1,000 (and that was a big one). Many of her small, 8x10 watercolors sell at auction in the $5,000 range. Her work is widely reproduced, and framed copies are often for sale in souvenir and gift shops in the region. She especially liked to paint snow scenes because the white paper itself would serve as the background.

THE PENNSYLVANIA DUTCH COUNTRY

There are many revivalist painters around today—modern artists who recreate or reinterpret traditional forms—some excellent, some of dubious quality. The most avidly collected revivalist is theorem (or stencil) painter and carver David Ellinger, whose work is usually colorful and highly decorative. Another contemporary, Barbara Strawser's work is also especially interesting.

The most characteristic and meaningful Pennsylvania Dutch folk art is fraktur. Fraktur are Americanized illuminated manuscripts. They can be either all hand done, or partially printed. For many they are the quintessential Pennsylvania German artifact, although like much "Dutch Stuff" they can also have been done in Virginia, Ohio, or Canada. Very much has been written about the meaning of fraktur, but usually we are dealing with documents outside of their natural context. Many of the finest surviving fraktur reached public collections a long time ago, having been gathered up by visionary pioneer collectors who acquired them cheaply from people like Nancy Risser's parents, who were quite consciously attempting to shake off their Dutch past.

The motifs on fraktur have been endlessly studied and debated. Applying the scholarly tools of the medievalist, some have assiduously sought to find meaning in every symbol, but the fact remains that unlike the rich traditional field of medieval iconography, there are few, and some say no, contemporary documents that can prove there is an iconic meaning to the decorations found on fraktur. A three-lobed tulip motif might represent the trinity, but it might also just be a pretty pattern.

Most of the motifs found on fraktur are a celebration of nature: flowers, vines, animals, and birds. These are usually combined with a few easily recognized symbols: hearts, crowns, angels, and compass stars. More unusual examples might include human representations, including soldiers. Very interestingly, the motifs found on fraktur are also often employed on painted furniture, pottery, textiles, and metalwork. Virtually any image found on fraktur can also be seen in a whole range of other crafts. Many are familiar with hearts and flowers on slip-decorated redware, but we can also find similar designs on a painted case made to hold a nineteenth-century bleeding device.

The earliest documented fraktur made in America was produced by the German Seventh Day Baptists, who established what is known today as the Ephrata Cloister. By the mid–1740s, these monastics were producing their distinctive fraktur that so closely resembles contemporary European penmanship. According to Corinne and Russell Earnest in *Fraktur: Folk Art and Family*, "Ephrata freehand fraktur approached perfection." The vast majority of fraktur, however, was made by and for members of the Lutheran and Reformed churches. Of the sectarians, the Mennonites and the Schwenkfelders were the most prolific creators of fraktur. Amish fraktur is also fairly abundant. Moravian fraktur was not very common and it has never been adequately studied. It is later, and more reminiscent of Victoriana, than is other fraktur. Christmas celebrations among the Moravians have always been splendid. Today tens of thousands of visitors are drawn to Bethlehem each year to see the elaborate seasonal decorations and the world-famed Putz or creche. Moravian Christmas traditions included exchanging small, freehand holiday texts that are considered to be among America's earliest Christmas cards. Also small, and among the most charming of the fraktur pieces made by the Pennsylvania Germans, are the small presentation pieces, usually love tokens that have been studied in preparation for a recent book by scholar Frederick S. Weiser, *The Gift is Small, the Love is Great*.

Fraktur made for Catholic families is rare, and many of the known examples were made near Bally in Berks County. On Catholic Taufscheinen (certificates of birth and baptism), special mention is usually made that the family was "Romish" or belonged to the "Romischen Relion." One fine example of Catholic fraktur is the Taufschein of Henrich Ley, born August 10, 1827, in Lebanon, which is attributed to Abraham Huth (active 1807–1830).

Jewish fraktur is well known in central Europe. The decorative motifs employed are similar to those of Christian ones, with some specifically Jewish inclusions like the menorah, the seven-branched candelabra that is one of the oldest and most important symbols of Judaism. The most common Jewish fraktur form is the Katuba, or marriage contract, and there are several active artists now creating this form for modern couples. Another well known fraktur form is the Mizrah, a wall ornament derived from the Hebrew word for "east," literally "the place of the shining [sun]," indicating the direction of prayer, which is always towards the site of the Temple in Jerusalem. Very little American fraktur can be documented as Jewish. There were, however, several Jewish penmen or dindamen who filled in blank taufscheinen or created bible entries for Pennsylvania German families. One Martin Wetzler commonly drew a Star of David on his works and signed his name in Hebrew. Justus I.H. Epstein (active 1873–1900) lived and worked in Reading for most of his career, just a few doors from his supplier of printed forms, The Eagle Bookstore.

Fraktur never died out completely. Among the Amish especially the craft has continued, and certainly by the 1920s early non-Amish revivalist craftspeople were making new documents in the old style. There are many craftspeople today who can provide you with a beautiful taufschein for your new baby. In recent years, as the value of antique fraktur has steadily risen, many fakes have come onto the market. For the novice, "buyer beware" is the ever important axiom.

Like hex signs, fraktur has entered the realm of modern tourism. There are many craftspeople who do pieces for sale in upscale gift shops and many framed reproductions are also available at more modest prices. As with hex signs, fraktur is used decoratively in many strange ways. There are always the coasters and the cocktail napkins, but there are also switch plates, lamp shades—even rolls of fraktur toilet tissue.

Pennsylvania Dutch textiles are very popular with visitors to the region, and many of the same motifs used on fraktur are also used historically to decorate all manner of the decorative arts from textiles to furniture to metals. Unfamiliar to many, but almost exclusively made by the Pennsylvania Dutch, is the show towel. The Germans themselves called the form "handtücher," more or less the equivalent of "hand towels." The Heritage Center Museum of Lancaster County owns an interesting piece that bears the legend *Maria Kreda Bersin hat das Hant Duch Gned in Yar 1795*, which translates, "Mrs. Maria Ber has made this hand towel in the year 1795." Maria, alas, had spelling problems. Twentieth-century collectors started calling these pieces "door towels" or "show towels," probably believing that "handtüch" implied a utilitarian rather than an ornamental nature. Whatever it is called, it is also an artifact on which the traditional motifs consistently appear. These long narrow towels were probably, on occasion, hung over the often soiled linen towel that was actually used to dry one's hands, when special company came. Show towels were "just for pretty" and could showcase the finest needle talents of an accomplished daughter or housewife. They were often hung on special pegs inserted into the backs of doors. A few handtücher are still being made by Mifflin County Amish. More privately the fine art of needlework and traditional concern for decoration could also be seen in pillow cases that were often beautifully embellished, as are the little known wall or privy bags hung on outhouse walls that the Dutch created. It is obvious that here too, as with the better known quilts, the towels, bed clothes, and privy bags that have survived in fine condition were only lightly or never used.

While some everyday quilts, like other textile forms, were made as a salvage craft, using bits and pieces of otherwise worn out clothing, most quilts were made of whole new cloth, usually purchased especially for the purpose. Patterns for some quilts followed traditional motifs, others were influenced by those appearing in contemporary women's magazines. Even among this latter group, inspired by popular culture, there is often a predilection towards the use of Dutch colors in Dutch combinations: yellows, greens, and reds on a white field in particular. Unlike many crafts, quilting never really died out among the Pennsylvania Germans and one can't really talk about a "revival," but perhaps a "resurgence." This has been triggered by many factors, most of which can also be applied to other areas, especially portions of West Virginia, where the quilting tradition is also very strong.

As a reaction to the modernism of the 1950s and 1960s, a taste for the country look emerged among many decorators, and then among homemakers. Quilts easily fit into the homey "look" that many craved. The bold patterns of many quilts were also very attractive for another reason. Strongly graphic quilt designs often presaged the techniques in the non-objective painting styles that became dominant in the 1940s and 1950s. This perhaps can explain the phenomenal popularity of early twentieth-century Lancaster County Amish quilts and the decidedly non-traditional craze for hanging quilts on the walls as works of art. Think of the work of abstractionists like Joseph Albers, Mark Rothko, Elsworth Kelly, or Kenneth Noland, and you can see the attraction of quilts in this light. If you are trendy, and not extraordinarily rich, a large highly graphic quilt hanging on your wall provided a very satisfactory substitute for an astronomically priced fashionable painting. That some modern painting had a textile feel is highlighted by an exchange between Georgia O'Keeffe and her assistant, potter Juan Hamilton. When looking at a Rothko, O'Keeffe said,

"Juan, these would make good rugs." "Don't you think Mr. Rothko would mind?" Juan asked. "I don't think so," the artist replied.

The practice of hanging quilts, unlike paintings, is detrimental to the textiles themselves and it is sad to realize that some of the most wonderful quilts ever made are stressed by hanging—a task they were never meant for—and they are being faded by exposure to too much bright light. On the market and in museums, quilts that are brightest and freshest are the most valued. These same quilts survived in that marvelous condition because they were seldom, if ever, used and lived most of their existence carefully tucked away in blanket chests. There are many collectors and owners of family treasures, however, who continue to carefully coddle their heirlooms. Fortunately for collectors, the Amish do not have a penchant for antiques and consider the possession of old objects that shouldn't be used as hochmütt or inappropriate pride.

Very significant to the great appreciation now accorded quilts and other needlework is the rise of the women's movement. "Women's work," once easily dismissed, was now to be greatly applauded. This new admiration gave extra impetus to traditional quilters and attracted many new craftswomen into the fold. The quilt sale sponsored by the Mennonite Central Committee held each year at the Farm Show Complex in Harrisburg is a showcase for quilts and a testimony to the liveliness of the crafts. Thousands of quilts appear at each show varying from pedestrian copies of old forms to completely modern designs. The workmanship also varies from the competent to the superb. The prices quilts fetch range from hundreds to tens of thousands of dollars each.

Driving along Lancaster County roads near the quaintly named town of Intercourse, one sees dozens of quilt shops, some on Amish farms operated by Amish women. Mennonite women are especially active in the business. The low end of the market is threatened today because of cheap quilt imports from China—once again, buyers beware. On a miniature, and much more modest, scale vintage pot holders can often have the graphic appeal of the quilt. Given their small size, these were indeed salvage art, as are pin cushions and rag rugs, many of which continue to be made, especially among the Amish and the Old Order Mennonites.

Furniture, in the Dutch tradition, was used in different quantities and varieties than among the English. While much furniture was made out of

Continued on page 101

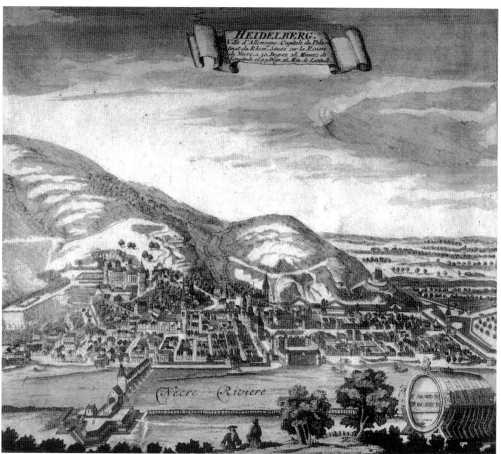

Heidelberg, Germany, as it appeared in the eighteenth century. Many, if not most, normative Pennsylvania Dutch trace their ancestry to the Palatinate die Pfalz, whose principal port, Heidelberg, was a starting point for many an emigrant's journey.

The Ephrata Cloister complex in Lancaster County retains strong medieval German echoes. Built in the 1740s under the charismatic leadership of Conrad Beissel (1690–1768), it housed religious orders devoted to perfection and the celebration of God and his works. Left to right, the surviving buildings are the Almonry (or Alms House), the Saal (church), and the Saron (Sister's House).

The Amish and Mennonites are, to the popular mind, the quintessential Pennsylvania Dutch; but in reality, they are just a small fraction of the Dutch. The building with "Welcome" on it was Lancaster's old City Hall. It is now part of the Heritage Center Museum of Lancaster County. The Central Market, built in the 1880s, is visible at the right.

Broad St., at Christmastime, Bethlehem, Pa.

Many of America's Christmas customs can be traced to Moravian introductions. Bethlehem, a tourist destination, prides itself as the "Christmas City." Bethlehem is visited in December for its Christmas Mart, its concerts, its lights, and its Putz (or creche).

Barn raisings are mythic events in Dutch country. Today they are associated exclusively with the Amish, but in earlier years, as seen in this Lancaster County photograph, most Dutch helped their neighbors to build new barns or rebuild damaged ones.

Two Dutch mechanics, probably brothers, posed in their overalls at the Schrempel Studio in South Bethlehem, c. 1905. The setting is a studio backdrop. Note that many workers wore collared shirts and ties in the early twentieth century.

VALENTINE HEISER

AUTOMOBILE

Repairing a Specialty

All Kinds of Machinery, Engines and
Gasoline Engines Repaired

Machinist and Plumber

Also Pipes and Supplies

Opposite Lutheran Church
ORWIGSBURG, PA.

When the automobile appeared in Dutch country, it was often serviced by your local machinist and plumber, or perhaps the local blacksmith. Valentine Heiser, who advertised, "Automobile Repairing a Specialty," had his shop across from the Lutheran Church in Orwigsburg in Schuylkill County.

Four young ladies and a pet dog pose in front of the garden of their farm home. Note the high picket fence, typical of the region. Many families first built a modest one-story house. When they could afford it, a larger home was added to the front.

Nature is not always kind in Dutch country. Occasional tornadoes occur, especially in parts of Berks and Lehigh Counties. This c. 1905 card shows a farmhouse in semi ruin after an ill wind blew. The large amount of debris suggests that a shed or small barn was also destroyed. Note all the people. Then, as now, everyone wanted to get into the picture.

Floods and ice dams destroyed low-lying farms. This Lancaster scene, c. 1905, was processed by G.H. Werntz of 23 East Orange Street in Lancaster, who sold "Cameras, Chemicals & Supplies."

Log houses are an important contribution of Dutch culture to American architecture. The early nineteenth-century Bobb House belongs to the Historical Society of York County and is open as a museum.

Death memorial photographs are unusual among the Dutch. The inscription on this stone reads:

FATHER
WINFIELD W. LIGHT
BORN JAN 12, 1871,
DIED JUNE 7, 1894
AGED
23 YEARS, 4 MO. 25 DA.
TEXT PSALMS 62-7.

Light (Licht) is a very common Dutch name. Notice the traditional German farm in the background. The banner on the grave reads, "OUR BROTHER."

The Golden Plough Tavern of 1741 is log downstairs and half timbered, or fachtwerk, above. Next to it is the 1751 German stone house that was used by General Horatio Gates when the capital of the United States was in York. Both buildings are now museums.

Dutch and British Island architecture melded very early. This building, traditionally called the Daniel Boone Homestead, near Birdsboro, Berks County, was built by English Quakers and Dutch of Huguenot descent. The section to the right was probably built 1752–1755 by William Maugridge. Famed frontiersman Daniel Boone was born on the site in 1734 in a log house built by his father, which was moved or destroyed. Johannes DeTurk then built on the foundation, completing the stone house as it appears today.

Homestead of Mordecai Lincoln, Lorane, Penn'a.,
Great-Great Grandfather of President Abraham Lincoln. Built 1733.

While the Lincoln House is essentially English, the barn is German in form. Still standing and in excellent condition, the Berks County farmstead is privately owned. This postcard was photographed and published by H. Winslow Fegley (1870–1944), a Dutchman very proud of his heritage and the Dutch country's Lincoln connection.

This Pennsylvania German bank barn is decorated with hex signs and a slogan reading, "Kempton Farm Museum." The structure was used to display antique farm implements used by the Dutch.

Every country crossroads town had its general store that was part business and part home. H.L. Gross's store in Centre Valley carried groceries, patent medicines, cloth, farm utensils, and "most everything you needed." Mail order and the automobile doomed the general store and turned survivors into "country stores," i.e., quaint tourist attractions.

As an agricultural people, the Dutch introduced many nature-related customs to the new world, including the myth of the Easter Bunny. This earliest known American rendition of the Easter Rabbit was probably made in Brunswick Township, Berks County, by artist Conrad Gilbert (1734–1812). Also a practical people, the Dutch viewed the real rabbit as a potential destroyer of crops. The only good rabbit was a cooked one served for dinner. (Abby Aldrich Rockefeller Folk Art Museum.)

Looking like an oversized elf, Laurence Gieringer towers overs the Lilliputian Dutch countryside he created in the first half of the twentieth century. Still an active tourist attraction, it is open 365 days a year.

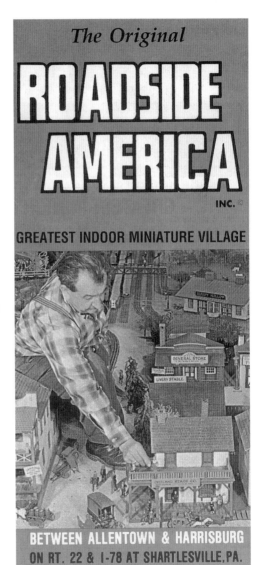

The Original

ROADSIDE AMERICA

INC. ©

GREATEST INDOOR MINIATURE VILLAGE

BETWEEN ALLENTOWN & HARRISBURG ON RT. 22 & I-78 AT SHARTLESVILLE, PA.

An engraving that appeared on the title page of an herbarium published in Frankfurt in 1546 shows a gardener attending to a raised bed surrounded by stakes that are identical to those still used in traditional Pennsylvania Dutch gardens.

A view of the re-created Dutch garden at the Landis Valley Museum in Lancaster County. Protestants often placed an Adam and Eve plant (Yucca filamentosa) in the center of the garden, as here. Catholics used a potted rosemary plant.

Noodles are a staple of Dutch cookery, but they apparently were not universally loved. One irate husband so disliked noodles that he threatened to dump them on his wife if she cooked them again. She did, and so did he! The incident was recalled by artist Lewis Miller, himself the son of eighteenth century German immigrants. (York County Heritage Trust.)

Cabbage was perhaps the most widely used vegetable the Dutch grew. Indeed, the Pennsylvania Germans were often called "The Sauerkraut Yankees" because of their love of the fermented vegetable. Fantasy postcards like this one were common in the first half of the twentieth century.

Tobacco raising was very important among the Dutch. One Eliza Gochnauer, at age 92, was proud of her crop on her traditional farm. Very labor intensive, the once profitable crop was especially popular with Amish and Mennonite farmers. Once the tobacco stalks were cut by hand they were threaded onto laths and hung in a special tobacco barn to dry. Afterwards, the leaves were stripped from the stems, graded by size, and baled.

The countryside near Allentown had several large duck farms. The Dutch not only enjoyed eating roast duck on special occasions, but visiting the farms was a favorite Sunday afternoon excursion for nearby city dwellers.

Harvest Service was often celebrated in Lutheran and Reformed churches before the Second World War. This c. 1910 altar was decorated with the fruits of harvest supplied by local farmers. The custom is now being revived, with the produce today more often coming from suburban back yards rather than farms.

Central Pennsylvania is the heartland of American chocolate making. Hershey Chocolate is headquartered in Dauphin County, Kline Chocolate (now part of M&M Mars) is in Elizabethtown in Lancaster County, Wilbur's "Home of the Wilbur Bud" is in Lititz, and Godiva Chocolates are made in Reading in Berks County.

Dairying is still a viable industry in Dutch country. The milk from these Holsteins on a Hershey farm found its way into the company's famed milk chocolate.

Alles os du esse kannst . . .

Pennsylvania Dutch Family Style Dinner
served daily 11:00 A.M. to 7:30 P.M.
SHARTLESVILLE HOTEL, SHARTLESVILLE, PENNA.

Beginning in the 1930s, a Berks County innkeeper started to appeal to tourists with his all-you-can-eat, or Alles os du esse kannst, family-style dinners featuring seven sweets and seven sours. The Shartlesville Inn lasted until the 1990s. Haag's Hotel, a little newer and down the street, still exists, serving its traditional fare.

Pennsylvania Dutch fraktur. This birth record is attributed to Samuel Bentz (1792–1850). Bentz, who worked in Northern Lancaster County, was a schoolmaster, as were many fraktur artists. Ladies with parasols are unusual on fraktur, but it was no doubt hoped that Lydia Glätz would be an elegant lady. Eventually, the surname was probably Anglicized to "Glass." (Heritage Center Museum of Lancaster County.)

Quilting has never died out among the Dutch. Here quilters, including several Mennonite ladies (note the prayer veils), demonstrate their craft at a festival in Hershey. Many Mennonite groups earn a great deal of money for their missionary quilting endeavors.

A carved and painted eagle fashioned by Wilhelm Schimmel (1817–1890) is an avidly collected folk object. Born in Hesse-Darmstadt in Germany, Schimmel spent most of his adult life near Carlisle in Cumberland County. The eagle was, perhaps, his most common subject and it is also a form that many revivalists re-create. (Cumberland County Historical Society.)

The Easter egg tree is a German tradition that was transplanted into Dutch country, where outdoor "Easter trees" are still common. More elaborate is this "Easter Tree Putz," which belonged to the Gaumer family of Allentown, whose display proudly contains over 1,000 eggs and related items.

Stoneware came in many forms, but none are more graceful than pitchers. The larger ones were used to serve beer, buttermilk, lemonade, or other beverages and were probably made in Philadelphia by Henry H. Remmy (1794–1878). The smallest pitcher bears the incised and pigmented inscription, "Elizabeth, 1890," and was, no doubt, a birthday present.

The Brunnersville Iron Foundry in Lancaster County was in business for over 150 years, making household utensils like kettles and skillets. In later years, they made tourist items like bullfrog door stops. Their casting techniques were timeless.

Jacob Zook (1915–2000), "The Hex Man of Paradise," worked in Paradise, on the tourist strip, in Lancaster County. He is hanging a "Rain" sign on his sales shed. Get out the umbrella! Zook produced many unique hex signs designed to ward off evil and bring good fortune.

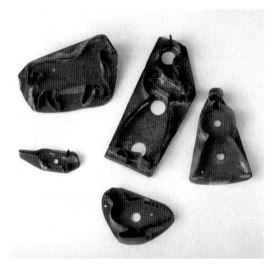

Cookie cutters let a tinsmith's imagination run wild. Many families had a dozen or more cutters, amassed over the years. Shaped cookies were especially popular at Christmas. Illustrated here are a basic woman, a female fishmonger, a bird, and, most unusual of all, a rat. The horse belonged to Esther Suzanna Steigerwalt (1885–1983) of Schuylkill County, who said of it, "Ach! That one! The legs always break."

Many revivalist craftsmen make and paint "tinware" or "toleware." The commercially made frying pan, brightly decorated, bears the legend, "Souvenir of Ephrata, Lancaster County 1949." It is early tourist ware. The tray outdoes any original piece in being "Dutchy." The design is clearly one inspired by fraktur—but greatly magnified. (Heritage Center Museum of Lancaster County.)

Clockmaker Martin Schreiner (1769–1866) used this gear-cutting machine and clockmaker's hammer over his long career in Lancaster County. He numbered all of his clocks—the highest known number is 431. (Edward F. Jr. and Virginia A. LaFond, and Heritage Center of Lancaster County.)

This slant front desk, inscribed "Jacob 1834 Maser," was made the year he married Catherine Christ. It is typical of the highly decorated furniture made in the Schwaban Creek Valley that was settled by Lutheran and German Reformed Church members in 1776. (Henry F. duPont Winterthur Museum.)

The ceiling of the Kershner Parlor, or stube, near Wernersville, was decorated by a Hessian soldier whose labor was sold to a local farmer. The interior, now at the Winterthur Museum, is furnished with fine Dutch pieces that enhance the baroque ceiling ornamentation. (Henry Francis duPont Winterthur Museum.)

Daniel Rose (1749–1827), painted by Jacob Witman (d. 1798), was a very successful Pennsylvania Dutch clockmaker working in Reading. An officer in the Continental Army and a state legislator, Rose had the reputation of being a dandy. His portrait, painted c. 1795, shows him surrounded by musical instruments, the symbols of a cultured gentleman. (The Historical Society of Berks County.)

Colonial portraits of the Pennsylvania Dutch are extremely rare. The only portraitist to have done a number of likenesses was Johann Valentine Haidt (1700–1780), a Moravian who painted his co-religionists. Shown here are John Jacob Schmick and Johanna Ingerheidt Schmick, missionaries to the Native Americans, in Bethlehem c. 1754. (The Moravian Historical Society, Nazareth.)

Cherry Hill School in Lancaster County is in the heart of the Dutch Belt. Here in 1923, Mennonite, Lutheran, and Reformed children attended the same one-room schoolhouse.

Ben Salem Lutheran and Reformed Church, a "Union Church" shared by Lutheran and Reformed congregations, is located in East Penn Township, Carbon County. It is the ancestral church of the regional Steigerwalt family. The picture showing Pastor William Strauss was taken in 1912.

Store-bought clothing and furniture changed the look of country people and their homes, and most aspired to look modern and up to date. Note the stylish furniture the smart-looking couple were looking at. In small towns throughout Dutch country, furniture sellers were also undertakers—because once they had been the cabinet makers who also made coffins.

Steigerwalt albums are filled with group pictures of large families. The Moses Steigerwalt family poses for a professional photographer, probably with a barn wall for a background, c. 1915.

Daniel Kressley (left) went off to the Civil War as a teenager. Surviving the Battle of Antietam, he returned home, married, and had a large family. He and his wife are surrounded by their eight adult children in a group portrait (below) photographed c. 1918. Esther Suzanna "Mama," who was by then married to Frank Steigerwalt, kneels at the right.

The Ambrose Stahler Steigerwalts pose for an informal snapshot on the farm while eating watermelon, c. 1925.

"Inside of the old Lutheran Church in 1800, York, Pa.," by folk artist Lewis Miller (1795–1882), shows the interior arrangement of an early church. There were two doors and cross aisles. Note the stove used to heat the interior, the wine-glass pulpit, and the organ built by Moravian Organ maker David Tannenberg (1728–1804). (Historical Society of York County.)

Henry Melchior Mühlenberg (1711–1787) is widely celebrated as the "Patriarch of the Lutheran Church in America," and he was responsible for the building of several churches. The oldest, and best preserved, of these is the Augustus Church at Trappe. Mühlenberg is buried in its church yard.

Gotthilf Henry Ernest Muhlenberg (1753–1815), painted by artist Jacob Eichholtz, was the most scholarly of Henry Melchior Mühlenberg's sons. For 35 years, he served as pastor of Holy Trinity Lutheran Church in Lancaster and was also the first president of Franklin College. He is best remembered today as a pioneer American botanist. (Phillips Museum of Art, Franklin and Marshall College.)

The Bethany Orphans' Home in Womelsdorf (above) served Reformed Church orphans who were expected to work on the institution's farm (below).

Mailed in 1922 to the Reverend Ira Gass in West Milton, the obverse of this card thanks the "Ref. Congregation" for "91 1/2 qts canned fruit veg. & jellies." Regional churches were encouraged to donate home preserved foods for "poor and unfortunate orphans."

The Amish and some Old Order Mennonites still maintain the one-room schoolhouses that were normative in rural America. This one is in Lancaster County.

THE BIRTHPLACE OF HON. JOSEPH HIESTER,
BERN TOWNSHIP, BERKS COUNTY, PA.
Born Nov. 18, 1752. Died June 10, 1832. Governor
of Pennsylvania 1820-1823.

Joseph Hiester (1752–1832) served a single term as governor from 1820 to 1823. The son of a prosperous Westphalian (Germany)-born father, Hiester was born in Bern Township, Berks County.

BIRTHPLACE OF HON. JOHN ANDREW SCHULZE,
STOUCHSBURG, PA.
Built 1770. Used as Parsonage by Christ Lutheran Church. Governor of
Pennsylvania 1823-1829. Born July 19, 1775. Died Nov. 18, 1852.

John Andrew Schulze (1775–1852), who was a two-term governor (1823–829), was born in Stouchsburg in Berks County where his birthplace is still owned by the Lutheran Church in this very well-preserved Dutch town.

Samuel Whitaker Pennypacker (left), who served as governor from 1903–1907, was a scholar devoted to his Dutch roots. A liberal Republican like Theodore Roosevelt, he was able to have the President be the keynote speaker when Pennsylvania's new State Capitol (below) was dedicated October 4, 1906. (Pennsylvania State Archives.)

Ray Shafer, who served as governor from 1967–1971, was an effective modern politician who knew that a handsome family could help win elections. He helped to shape a new Pennsylvania constitution, adopted in 1968.

ELECT RAY SHAFER GOVERNOR

Janie   Diane   Ray Shafer   Jane Shafer   Phil   Marcia   Flip

Dwight David Eisenhower, hero of World War II and President of the United States, was born in Kansas of Pennsylvania German ancestry. While President, he and his wife bought the only home they ever owned—outside of Gettysburg. The farmhouse is now a museum.

Many Pennsylvania politicians in our pluralistic society might have strong Dutch roots and a name belonging to another ethnic group. State Senator Joe Conti (b. 1954) is a case in point. His maternal grandmother was born Stella Freed Nice. She was the daughter of Wilson Nice, who is buried in the Franconia Mennonite Cemetery. Proud Grandma Stella, whose married name was Murray, "lived from July 15, 1899 to July 21, 1997—just missed 100." She is shown here holding future Senator Conti (below) in 1955.

"Pennsylvania Dutch Stuff"

Continued from page 60

abundant fine local hardwood, including walnut and cherry, the furniture often most desired and collected today is made of softwood, especially pine and tulip poplar, painted and frequently embellished with fraktur-like decoration. It often employed imagery drawn from nature, with stylized carnations, tulips, birds, and trailing vines sharing space with mystical creatures like angels and unicorns.

The traditional Dutch home, as explained earlier, used few chairs. Usually only the father would have a chair at the dining table. By custom, women and children sat on benches, many of whose bases are cut with baroque curves. In many houses, benches were also built into one corner of the kuche. The most common chairs were the plank-backed brettstuhl or peasant chair and the ladderback. An extraordinary brettstuhl made for the Christian Stauffer family of Lancaster County has a compass decoration on its back that matches the rare plaster decoration on the ceiling of the eighteenth-century house's stube.

As years went on, many Dutch craftsmen made Windsor chairs. While the Windsor form is clearly English in origin, German-made Windsors often have broader seats than those made in other regions as well as distinctive turnings. By the mid-nineteenth century, many Dutch homes would own sets of plank bottom chairs and even settees. Beds, traditionally piled high with mattress-ticks, down comforters, sheets, quilts, and bolsters and pillows, were usually simple. By the post–Civil War years, many houses were furnished with fashionable factory-made furniture. The carefully restored Landis brothers' home at the Farm Museum is a wonderful example of a farmhouse in transition from the age of handcraft to the time of the factory.

The most impressive piece of kitchen furniture that a prosperous family might have was the kitchen dresser or "Dutch cupboard." This large piece with its closed cupboards at the base, and its open shelves—or glazed cabinet tops—was used to display the family's best glass, pottery, china, silver, and pewter. Grained pieces are common. Highly decorated pieces are rare because you didn't want to detract from the items being displayed. Less affluent families would content themselves with hanging cupboards. Some of the best of these had a built-in spoon rack where treasured silver, pewter, or horn utensils could be displayed.

THE PENNSYLVANIA DUTCH COUNTRY

The chest or kist is the most readily identifiable piece of Pennsylvania Dutch furniture. Usually given to teenage girls, and less often boys, the chest would be their own private space within the often crowded interiors of German households. It was not uncommon for a chest owner to paste his or her taufshein (birth and baptism certificate) in the inside lid of the chest. Many lids retain tack holes on the inside where more transient treasures might also have been attached. A small till, inside the chest, could hold small items of clothing or special trinkets. Chests of drawers were very slow in gaining favor among the Pennsylvania Dutch, many of whom, well into the twentieth century, preferred to use the kist for clothing storage. Going to many sales in the 1960s and 1970s, the last period when large numbers of traditional households were being broken up, one would often see four to six kisten come out of an old farm house to every chest of drawers.

Most chests were plain, made of a softwood, usually pine or tulip poplar, the sturdy but ugly hardwood Dutch craftsmen often used. Most were simply painted. Some chests, showing English influence, might have a single drawer or a row of three drawers along the bottom. They would also be fitted with fashionable English-style brass pulls. Simple bracket feet were the most common, rather than the ball feet of their homeland antecedents. For the antiques collector, the most desirable chests are the elaborately decorated ones, especially those given to girls, which are often dated and usually bear the recipient's name or initials. The decoration on the most sought after of chests is very much like that on fraktur. One might also expect that fraktur artists could have decorated chests. This was certainly the case with William Otto (1761–1841), who made fraktur and also decorated chests with similar motifs. Examples of his work, done in Schuylkill County, date from 1834 to 1840. Some chest decorators, like the Selsers (or Seltzers) of Jonestown, had as distinctive styles as the best fraktur artists and they often signed their work. Dutch chests were usually decorated on three sides and on the lid as well, Unworn, or lightly worn tops are rare, and especially desirable to collectors and, of course, come out of very unusual homes where they were always covered and/or seldom used for the resting of objects.

The most desirable and luxurious furniture form that the traditional Dutch family would own was the shrank or wardrobe. Occasionally it was delineated as the "*kleidershrank*"—or clothing wardrobe. The shrank is similar in form to the Holland Dutch kas (a name some mistakenly apply to the Pennsylvania German furniture form) and to the ubiquitous French-denominated "armoire" (variants of which hide hundreds of thousands of television sets).

If you owned a shrank, it would be kept in the best room, the stube (or stove room) or parlor where it stood as a testimony to your affluence. Most shranken were paneled and made of hardwood, usually walnut, others were made of softwood and elaborately painted. For many of today's collectors, the most desirable, and rarest shranken, are those made with sulphur inlay in walnut. The most famous and extraordinary of these pieces is the Huber shrank made in Lancaster County, which is now in the collection of the Philadelphia Museum of Art. English-influenced pieces, here as in the kist, often have a drawer or drawers along the bottom and use English-styled brass pulls. The most traditional of pieces often have ball feet, while bracket or ogee feet are not uncommon. The interior of the shrank is usually fitted with wooden hanging hooks for clothing. Many are fitted one-half for hanging and half with shelves. Others contain all shelves.

Distinguishing the Pennsylvania German shrank from the Holland Dutch kas is that, blessedly, shranken are made so they can be easily disassembled for moving. Some great shranken have been described in auction notices as "a big wardrobe found in the attic," often their fate when fashion relegated them to a mere utilitarian role. A few especially rare shranken can be traced to the specific historic houses for which they were made. These pieces might share matching profiles with the moldings of the room in which they originally stood.

Revivalist craftsmen, like pioneer Clyde Stacks of Palmyra, Lebanon County, who died in 1987, often embellished plain older pieces with his distinctive variation of Dutch design. Stacks, a long-time industrial arts teacher at the Milton Hershey School, learned the craft from an antiques dealer friend while he was still a student at Franklin and Marshall College in Lancaster. Ed Long often took his young protegee to visit the Landis brothers at their farm where he could see and study original historic pieces with their paint intact. The Landis farm is today the Landis Valley Farm Museum, a treasure trove of Pennsylvania Dutch artifacts. The Landis brothers, George (1867–1954) and Henry (1865–1956) were both well educated engineers who had had careers in New York City. When they returned to their ancestral farm, they saw the culture of their childhood disappearing before their eyes, and they set about collecting huge quantities of obsolete artifacts that no one else wanted.

Many of Clyde Stacks's early decorated pieces were very close to their prototypes and many have entered into the antiques market as old pieces. A chest once owned by Frank Sinatra and pictured in a magazine spread was a Stacks piece that had found its way to Southern California. Later, on his own, Clyde developed his own style and almost always signed his works. He brought color and verve to many pedestrian items, including chests, dry sinks, hanging cupboards, and buckets. He taught the craft to his daughter-in-law Wendy Stacks. His son David is an expert furniture restorer whose speciality is the re-creation of antique finishes. David recently restored all 230 of the historic desks in the Pennsylvania House of Representatives' Chamber in the State Capitol at Harrisburg. As a new sideline, David is now often asked to restore pieces his father painted.

Today there are many revivalists at work making and painting reproduction Dutch spinning wheels, footstools, benches, chests, and especially miniature chests. Their work, in widely varying quality, is offered in retail outlets all through Dutch country.

The Dutch also used wood for many other commonplace items. Burls were avidly sought and carved into strong, lightweight bowls. Other bowls were made from blocks of solid wood. Wood was used for spoons, butter paddles, butter marks, mangle boards, and springerle molds as well as spinning wheels and looms—items all commonplace to the everyday life of the Dutch. Mangle boards were used to smooth bed linens. Springerle molds are still used to make the highly decorated anise flavored Christmas cookies that have been a Dutch tradition for generations.

One pair of unique wooden utensils rarely seen today was used when down was harvested. Because the best quality down is collected from living geese, the birds protested the procedure. The unfortunate bird would be caught and its beak clamped with a special device. Next, the bird would be placed in another restraint that kept its neck rigid, prevented its wings from flapping, and exposed its breast for plucking. The immobilized bird was placed into a specially shaped, narrow-necked basket and plucked. The narrow neck kept the down from floating away.

Additionally, wood was used to make baskets, which were a necessity in the pre-plastic age. The Germans used osier willow for many baskets. Shrubs were specially trimmed to provide the long, straight branches that were used for weaving. The most desirable baskets were those made of split oak—especially woven into the arshenbach or buttocks form that rests sturdily on flat surfaces. The buttocks basket is the perfect Pennsylvania German artifact because it fits so well with the barnyard and bathroom humor so typical of the Germans. Another highly prized basket form used rounded oak strips formed by forcing splints through a die.

Supplementing wood was coiled rye grass, often woven with splints of supple hickory wood. Rye grass was especially favored for bread and storage baskets, and for bee hives. The reason for using rye grass is that natural toxins in the stalks ward off many insects. Rye grass was often used for down baskets as well. It was baleful to the poultry mites that had to be cleaned from down before mattresses or feather beds were made. And of course, rye grass was a byproduct of a favored Dutch food crop. Frugal Germans even continued to thatch their barns with straw into the early twentieth century. Rye straw–thatched hay ricks lasted even longer. While basketmaking never completely died out among the Dutch, it was certainly in decline before the 1960s. Revival craftsmen now produce myriad baskets in willow, oak, and rye grass. By their very nature, baskets were consumed. Very few dateable early nineteenth-century or earlier baskets survive.

On a more frivolous note, woodcarving, or whittling, was a favored pastime among the Pennsylvania Dutch. Carvings of toys or figures were highly prized. Some carvers are known by name, many others are anonymous, but their tradition is an ancient one on both sides of the Atlantic.

Among the finest of the carvers was German-born Wilhelm Schimmel (1817–1890) of Cumberland County, whose many surviving figures reflect a very Germanic sensibility. An alcoholic, Schimmel did many of his works for food, drink, or permission to spend a few nights in a hayloft. A surprising number of these figures still belong to descendants of those for whom they were carved. Schimmel died in the Cumberland County Alms

House. There are many revivalists at work, many of whom reproduce or are influenced by his work. Others often reflect the work of John Reber (1851–1937) of Lehigh County.

Pottery was a housewares necessity. Most Dutch kitchen crockery was made locally using a widely available material, red clay—the same material used in brick making. Redware was commonplace in the homelands as well, and unlike fashionable imported tablewares, such as tin-glazed earthenware (delft) and china, this craft did not require either specialized materials or extraordinary skills in manufacture. Clay was dug and worked most easily during the spring, thrown or molded and dried during the summer, and fired in fall and winter. Almost every Dutch community of any size probably had a potter, most of whose products were strictly utilitarian. Jars, pots, plates, pie pans, and jugs would have been the bulk of his manufacture. The most widely used glaze was transparent with a lead oxide base. Color was added by combining other metals and their salts with the glaze. Manganese gave browns and copper fillings made green. Jugs and jars were turned on a wheel, while dishes and pie pans were made of clay that had been formed with a rolling pin and then shaped over molds. Redware figurines were either made freehand or occasionally formed in hinged molds.

While still wet, some pieces were decorated with simple incised bands or borders. Most, however, were left plain and air dried to the "leather" state, after which they were glazed. If an item was to be used for dry storage or as a pie pan, it only needed to be glazed on the inside—thus conserving lead oxide. Most pieces of redware were finished with a clear lead oxide glaze or with a chocolate-colored manganese brown glaze. Often a clear glaze streaked with brown was used. Another popular decorative form required "slip," a thin white clay. Slip was put in a "slip pot," a device that looked like an inkwell, but with one to three or even five spouts made of sharpened quills. The slip, which appears yellow under lead oxide glaze, was trailed on the unbaked clay form and allowed to dry before the final finish was applied.

The most eagerly collected redware pottery is decorated sgriffito. Here the entire surface was covered with white slip, which was allowed to set. The slip was then scraped away to show a red pattern beneath. Many of these were presentation pieces and were seldom used. Designs, like those on fraktur, were predominantly floral folk motifs, but items with animal and human decorations, inscriptions, and often humorous mottos are also well known. A famed plate bears the German motto, "I cook what I like, what the dog won't eat, my husband will!" Redware was cheap and useful, but it was also very breakable and the lead glaze made it unsuitable for use with acidic foods that would leach the lead from the pottery. Lead poisoning was recognized very early as a disease. The first medical text published in America was on that disease. Redware would eventually be supplanted by glass and stoneware pottery. Except for flowerpots, and occasional figurines, very little utilitarian redware was made after 1880. Craftsmen began reviving the redware tradition as early as the 1920s. In the post–World War II years, craftsman revival redware became very common. The beginnings of the mainstream redware revival might well have begun with Russell R. Stahl (*d.* 1986), the last of a line of potters, whose shop was located in Lehigh County's Powder Valley. After World War II, Stahl had returned home with no intention of assuming his ancestral trade. But with no job prospects in his home town, he resumed a pre-war apprenticeship with his father, Isaac Stahl (*d.* 1950). Others followed him on his revival trail. One of these, James Christian Seagreaves (1913–1997), began experimenting on his rear porch in Alburtis in 1948. Seagreaves's only real teacher was an itinerant Greek potter named George Karras, who gave him a number of technical pointers. In 1951 Seagreaves built a pottery shop on busy Route 222 in Breinigsville, between Allentown and Kutztown. His wares were usually traditional, but sometimes with a modern feel. Today, the many talented craftsmen working in the field include Ned Foltz and Lester Breininger.

The demand for a more durable pottery was answered by the manufacture of stoneware. Salt-glazed stoneware was probably developed in the Rhineland in the early middle ages, and most early pieces of the pottery were imported. Large-scale production of stoneware couldn't begin until improved transportation made it possible to easily ship the white clay needed for its manufacture. Much white clay came from Amboy, New Jersey, or Long Island, New York; the brown clay or "Albany slip" for lining the vessels came from the upper Hudson Valley of New York. Stoneware is vitreous and even without glazing is substantially waterproof. Because of its strength, it is possible to make larger storage jars of stoneware than of redware; thus stoneware jars could even replace some small wooden casks. While rarities like stoneware teapots, flasks, and even banks exist, most stoneware, which was often decorated with a simple cobalt blue design, was formed into crocks, jugs, canning jars, churns, and pitchers.

After being raised, usually on a wheel (marks of the potter's fingers are often clearly visible inside), stoneware was often decorated by turning a coggle wheel around the rim and applied handles were attached. Early stoneware was frequently decorated with incised flowers or birds. Later stoneware was almost exclusively decorated with blue pigment. Here again the conventional decorations were stylized flowers and birds, but representations of buildings, animals, and even people are known. Next, the piece was ready for the kiln into which, at the proper moment (when a very high temperature was reached), the potter would shovel common salt. The sodium in the salt vapors combined with silica in the clay to form a hard layer of sodium silicate—a virtually impermeable glaze.

Because of transportation and distribution advantages, south central Pennsylvania, with its large German population, became a center of stoneware production. After 1890, the making of stoneware became highly mechanized, and by World War I the handcraft element was virtually dead, a victim of new ceramic, metal, and glass technologies. Most German farms had crocks where fresh eggs were stored for winter use in water glass (a thick sodium silicate solution). These crocks, with their interiors characteristically discolored with the white water glass, are often seen. As a craft, the making of salt glaze pottery was revived much later than was redware production. There are a number of makers who are active today. The Pfaltzgraff Company of York, a manufacturer of contemporary tableware, is a descendent of Pennsylvania Dutch stoneware potters who can trace their history to the late eighteenth century.

Like all upwardly mobile peoples, the Dutch enjoyed imported goods, if they could afford them. Prosperous Pennsylvania Dutch farm families were a very promising market for potteries, many in Staffordshire, England, which turned out very colorful pottery to appeal to this specific market. "Gaudy Dutch," "Gaudy Welsh," and spatterware became so identified with the

Pennsylvania Germans that many people came to believe, erroneously, that the colorful pottery was made locally.

Less celebrated as a Dutch-specific imported tableware is oriental porcelain or china. By the mid-nineteenth century, it was widely available in Dutch country. One elderly Pennsylvania German woman with a marvelous collection of period blue and white china says that the pieces were bought by her great aunts in Reading, where the ladies "picked out the pieces with the darkest blue." The Schwenkfelder Museum in Pennsburg, has a large collection of orientalia brought back by various missionaries.

The most celebrated colonial American glass was made in Dutch country by German-born entrepreneur Henry William Stiegel (1729–after 1797), whose taste for high living earned him the nickname "Baron." Stiegel's glassworks were given a great stimulus by the non-importation agreements of the early 1770s. At their height, the Manheim Works, in Lancaster County, employed 130 craftsmen, including engravers, cutters, and enamelers. The enterprise, which began with great promise in 1763, went bankrupt in 1774.

While pottery and glass break easily, objects made of metals—iron, tin, copper, brass, silver, and even gold—survive in great quantity and in very many varieties. Central Pennsylvania was especially rich as a source of iron. "Baron" Stiegel, famous as a glassmaker, was also an ironmaster. His Mary Ann furnace produced the cast iron that would go to the bloomery to be converted into the wrought iron that blacksmiths needed. The furnace made the cast iron necessities of life: pots and kettles, firebacks, and stove plates. They also made military ordinance, including cannons and cannon balls. Stiegel and his fellow ironmasters—both Dutch and English—often embellished their stove plates with religious symbolism, leading the pioneer student of antique American iron Henry Chapman Mercer to call his 1914 epoch study of stoves and stove plates *The Bible in Iron*. The book's full title quite literally tells the whole story: *The Bible in Iron, or, The pictured stoves and stove plates of the Pennsylvania Germans, with notes on colonial fire-backs in the United States, the ten-plate stove, Franklin's fireplace and the tile stoves of the Moravians in Pennsylvania and North Carolina, together with a list of colonial furnaces in the United States and Canada.* Mercer, who would often reproduce early iron, favored German examples for his creations. German motifs were also used on his famous tiles made at Mercer's "Moravian Tile Works" in Doylestown, named in honor of the sectarians who were acclaimed for their Colonial-era ceramics. Today, the pottery at "Old Salem," a preserved Moravian center in North Carolina, produces many reproductions of early forms, including Moravian tile stoves.

It is surprising how many homely, everyday items were embellished and treated as aesthetic as well as utilitarian objects. Kitchen wares are a good example. Flesh forks, ladles, and spatulas were kitchen necessities along with cast iron pots, skillets, and trivets. Interestingly, the Germans did not traditionally use andirons. Pots and skillets are usually unembellished except for the caster's name. Trivets made of wrought iron, however, could be fanciful in form. Many were heart shaped. Flesh forks, ladles, and spatulas were often wedding presents and many are decorated with engraved hearts, tulips, and vines. Sometimes they bear the owner's initials or a name and date. Rare pieces are enriched with brass inlay, and some iron pieces have brass bowls or blades.

The Germans are justly famed for their decorative iron hinges, which often incorporated hearts, crowns, tulips, and ram's horn motifs. An especially interesting form is the "rat tail" hinge that is light and delicate as well as decorative. Among the most evocative artifacts are the tool boxes carried on Conestoga wagons. These small painted boxes usually were embellished with elaborate hinges and sometimes escutcheon plates as well. Not only containers, but the tools themselves were often beautiful in design and embellishment, no matter the function they were meant for. The form of a well-designed goose-wing broad axe is beautiful, in and of itself; any engraving is frosting on the cake. There are many craftsman revival blacksmiths at work today throughout Central Pennsylvania. One of the best is John D. Tyler of Newville.

Iron made into thin sheets in a rolling mill and then coated with tin was the basis of "white ware" or "tin ware." These objects were made by the "whitesmith." Tinware was prized for its shine and its smooth surface that could hold paint. Tinware was popular for fancy trays, coffee pots, and boxes. Some unpainted pieces were decorated with engraved and stippled designs. Painted surfaces often bore traditional designs. Craftsman revival tin wares of the post–World War II period are often "Dutchier" than the originals.

"Pennsylvania Dutch Stuff"

Tin was often shaped into fat lamps, lanterns, and sconces. The Germans, of course, made candles, often molded in tin molds and tin candlesticks, but most brass and pewter candlesticks, favored by the more affluent, were imported. As an agricultural people, the Germans used fat or betty lamps far longer than many groups. Whether made of tin or wrought iron, or occasionally of brass, fat lamps continued to be made at least until the 1850s. Lamps were often fitted with a hanger that allowed them to be suspended from a ledge like a fireplace mantle or the arm of a chair. Other lamps rested on lamp stands that look like oversized thread spools. Some of these pedestals were made of wood, but many were made of red clay. In the early 1900s, tinware slowly passed out of favor, replaced by enamel ware, aluminum, and stainless steel. Some rural tinsmiths made their livelihoods producing raised seam tin roofs until they, or their successors, were again rendered obsolete by the new inexpensive composite roof shingles. As early as the 1930s, a tinware revival began. Put on hold by World War II, the art of tinsmithing flourishes today. Most modern tin, with the exception of cookie cutters and perhaps table crumbers, used to lift crumbs from the table, tend to be relegated to ornament status, even if they replicate archaic implements like cheese molds. Tinware lighting devices, especially wall sconces and chandeliers, are especially popular among contemporary craftspeople and their customers.

Copper and its alloy, brass, were also important metals. Utilitarian copper, because of its heat conductivity, was used for making highly prized kettles, many of which are marked by their makers. Copper was also widely used in making measures, funnels, stills, and that most German of utensils, the apple butter kettle, which was a huge vessel used to make gallons of the prized sweet. Much smaller brass kettles were especially desired for jelly making, but the more expensive and harder to work metal was much less commonly used than copper. As mentioned earlier, brass was occasionally combined with iron in kitchen utensils and it was also used for making small decorative hinges. Brass was also employed by Pennsylvania German organ builders who were justly famed for their skills. Moravian organ builder David Tannenberg (1728–1804), a man of many trades (including cabinet maker and school master); and Conrad Doll (1772–1819) were especially important. Born in Saxony, Tannenberg was the son of parents born in Moravia. Greatly influenced by

Moravian leader Count von Zinzindorf, he was determined to emigrate to the New World. A joiner by trade, when he arrived in Bethlehem in 1765, he moved to Lititz where he would remain for the rest of his life, making about one organ a year. His organ building strongly influenced Conrad Doll, who had been born in Lancaster. Two of Doll's brothers were also craftsmen of note. His brother Joseph (*b.* 1768) was a clockmaker and silversmith, and Jacob (*b.* 1771) was a gunsmith. Astronomer David Rittenhouse (1732–1796) used brass, which is basically non-corrosive, to make the famed telescope he used for the transit of Venus observations in 1769. Rittenhouse, also a clockmaker, was skilled in working with the metal, which was the most common metal used for clockworks. Rittenhouse was only the most famous of many Pennsylvania German clockmakers. He was probably also the most assimilated of them. Others like the Hoffs and the Shreiners of Lancaster County took longer times to be affected by English modes.

Pewter was another commonly used metal. For the most part, pewter was used for tableware (plates, trays, beakers, spoons, coffee and tea pots), buttons, candlesticks, and communion services. Decoration was either cast or more rarely engraved. While much American pewter, unlike its continental counterpart, is very often unmarked, the nature of its molded construction gives the scholars clues to the maker. Any given craftsman had only a few molds and the parts cast from them were used interchangeably. Therefore, the stem of a candlestick and the stem of a chalice made by the same hand at the same approximate time would be identical.

Among the most important early pewterers in Pennsylvania was Philadelphia's German-born William Will (1742–1798) and central Pennsylvania's Johann Christian Heyne (1715–1781), who arrived in Philadelphia in 1742 on the ship *Catherine* as a member of the "First Sea Congregation" of the Moravian Church. In 1752, he and his wife Maria settled in Lancaster. Six months after Maria's death in 1764, Heyne married a widow, Anna Regina Steinmann, whose descendants would become, and remain, prominent newspaper owners. Several fine Pennsylvania German craftsmen led the pewter revival that has flourished since the end of World War II.

Pewter is essentially an alloy of tin and copper. Historically it contained traces of antimony and lead as well. New knowledge about metals has outlawed lead in the mix and given modern pewter a slightly different look and feel. Spectrographic analysis is a useful tool in determining the authenticity of a pewter object. There are two schools of thought concerning the appearance of pewter. Old pewter with a higher than present antimony content can take a remarkably high, silver-like polish; this is probably the way the Germans maintained it. Many antiquarians, however, prefer the dull gray patina that unpolished pewter acquires.

Pewter has always been expensive. It was the "second best" service in wealthy households and the very most fashionable churches, and the best in less affluent settings. Pewter melts at a low temperature, and putting old pewter in a modern dishwasher will distort its shape. Pewter that was badly dented or broken was seldom repaired, but rather melted down and recast. The making of pewter declined in the 1830s with the increased availability of reasonably priced glass and china and with the widespread introduction of silver plated base metal.

The phrases "silver and gold" and "Pennsylvania Dutch" are almost never used in the same sentence because these precious metals do not lend themselves to the quaint and folksy image many ascribe to the Pennsylvania Germans. And of course, farm towns and village crossroads did not support silversmiths. Some wealthy farmers joined urban merchants and professionals in commissioning objects of silver and gold, although much gold jewelry was probably imported. Prior to the establishment of trusted banks, silver money was often converted into identifiable silverware—marked trays, serving dishes, tea services, candlesticks—as protection from theft. One not only had excess wealth protected, but one could use it, openly, too. If feasible, silver was transformed locally so as not to be exposed to the dangers of shipment.

Most silver was marked by a maker's symbol or hallmark, mandatory in Europe, customary in America. Additionally, silver has a small content of copper added, necessary for its strength. But not until the adoption of "sterling" in the late nineteenth century was there a standard silver alloy. Silver is worked in two basic ways: casting and raising. Raising utilizes silver's special malleable quality and is used in the manufacture of bowls and teapots and the like. Starting with a flat piece of metal, a skilled craftsman using a small mallet strikes the silver repeatedly, causing it to "rise." After the piece is formed, the craftsman polishes away all visible tool marks. Silver ornamentation is often used to compensate for the varied qualities of the metal as well as to note its ownership. Silver is easily scratched; accordingly, trays are often chased and engraved so that scratches don't show. Because silver is a nearly perfect conductor of heat, teapots and coffee pot handles were insulated, as well as decorated with bands of ivory and exotic woods.

Among the most important German silversmiths were the Haverstick family and Peter Getz (1764–1809). The progenitor of the Haverstick clan was German-born Michael Haberstück. Two of his sons, William (1756–1823) and Matthias (1770–1810) were silversmiths as were William's three sons: William, Jr. (1780–1859), John (working in Lancaster, 1805–1809), and George (1788–1824). Getz is especially well known for the silver objects he made for wealthy Jewish land speculator Aaron Levy. Getz also made a medal honoring George Washington in 1792, which is now in the collection of the Smithsonian Institution. As a craftsman of many trades, Getz even made false teeth. Both Getz and the Haversticks, in addition to their table items, made silver and occasionally, perhaps, gold jewelry including shoe buckles, cuff buttons, and necklaces. These skilled craftsmen used many methods to expand their income, as this item from the December 9, 1797, *Lancaster Journal* shows:

WILLIAM HAVERSTICK
Goldsmith and Jeweller

Respectfully informs his friends and the public that he continues carrying on the Goldsmith and Jeweller's Business in its various branches, in the house of Mr. Frederick Heitz in King Street, East of the Court-House, opposite to Mr. John Hubley's where he has on hand a Large and Elegant Assortment of Gold and Silverware.

And, in addition to his Store, he has just received a very neat and well chosen assortment of Dry Goods and Groceries, with a variety of China, Glass and Queens Ware; all of which will be sold on the most reasonable terms.

He returns his sincere thanks to his friends and customers for their favours since he commenced business in this place, and hopes

for such future encouragement as his strict attention and punctuality
shall be found to merit

Silver and gold made by Dutch craftsmen is almost always made in the latest, i.e., English style for a fashionable clientele. Hence it is seldom, if ever, reproduced today.

While revivalist and reproduction Pennsylvania Dutch decorative arts and crafts can be seen almost everywhere, unless you are invited into the homes of collectors, you need to visit museums to see the best of Dutch material culture. The very best and most comprehensive collections of Pennsylvania Dutch "stuff" (to borrow from the title of the 1944 pioneer work by Earl F. Robacker, *Pennsylvania Dutch Stuff*) are at the Philadelphia Museum of Art and the Henry Francis duPont Winterthur Museum in Delaware. Thanks to Mr. duPont, there is even a substantial Pennsylvania German Collection at the American Museum in Bath, England.

The Dutch country itself is rich in collections of Pennsylvania German materials. The State Museum of Pennsylvania in Harrisburg has very good Pennsylvania German Collections. Also operated by the Pennsylvania Historical and Museum Commission are the Ephrata Cloister, the Conrad Weiser Homestead, and the Landis Valley Museum—all of which display Dutch stuff. The Berks County Historical Society in Reading, the Lancaster County Historical Society, and the Cumberland County Historical Society in Carlisle are important repositories, as are the Heritage Center Museum of Lancaster County, the Reading Public Museum, and the Phillips Museum of Franklin and Marshall College in Lancaster.

In a class by itself, thanks to the efforts of pioneer collector of Pennsylvania German materials and eccentric architect, Henry Mercer Chapman (1856–1930), is the Mercer Museum of the Bucks County Historical Society in Doylestown, Bucks County. Some museums like the Reading Public Museum have a broad collection; others like the Cumberland County Historical Society are especially rich in wood carvings. All are worth visiting. In Franklin County, the Renfrew Museum has an outstanding collection of redware pottery made by the Bell family, Dutch potters who worked in both Pennsylvania and Virginia.

Chapter Five

A DUTCH FAMILY

There is a fascination with the Amish, and there are various books about the Amish family and their community. Some of the best of these were written by the late John B. Hostetler (1918–2001). Born an Amishman, he "went gay" or "English" and became a Mennonite and an academic. His pioneering *Amish Society* has appeared in numerous editions, but there are no similar books about the church people—although there are many books about their institutions and their public lives. There are, of course, German families whose ancestors have been distinguished or famous through several generations, like the Muhlenbergs and the Wisters/Wistars, but there is very little exploration of a more typical family.

To fill a void, this chapter introduces the Steigerwalts of Central Pennsylvania—a family whose common ancestors arrived in America in 1767 and who have quietly lived and increased in America for almost 250 years.

As in other Dutch families, many Steigerwalts have a strong sense of tradition and a devotion to genealogy. Also, like many others, they hold family reunions. In common with other Dutch families, they have become so numerous that they often wear name tags, sometimes identifying their line of descent. There is a fascination in listening to the generations born 1880–1920, who all had, or still have, an intimate knowledge of their ancestors and who enjoyed discussing the intricacies of descent with the devotion of Talmudic scholars discussing Hebraic text.

The family's origin is in the Steigerwald region of present-day Germany, a hilly part of the Palatinate, not far from Heidelberg. Many of its inhabitants took a variant of their homeland as a name, when a surname was required: Steygerwaldt, Steigerwald, Steigerwalt, etc. As a result of this practice, there are Protestant, Catholic, and Jewish Steigerwalts.

The progenitors of the Pennsylvania Steigerwalts were Johann Frederich Steigerwalt (*b.* 1731) and his wife, Catherine Heuser (*b.* 1734), who emigrated from Fuerschbach-Hanau in the province of Alsace, arriving in Philadelphia October 26, 1767, on the ship *Britannia*. With them were their four sons: Johann "John," the eldest (*b.* 1758); Carl Otto (*b.* 1760); Johann Petrus "Peter," (*b.* 1762); and Andreas "Andrew," (*b.* 1764). A daughter, Maria Catherine, and two other sons, Johann Frederick II and Johann George "George," were born in America.

Unlike many of their countrymen, these Steigerwalts entered America as freemen, apparently able to pay their own way; but financial concerns forced them to indenture their seven-year-old son, Carl Otto, to a farmer in Greenwich Township, Berks County. Bound for 14 years, at 21 he was released from service and, following custom, received a suit of homespun, a pair of shoes, and stockings.

Indentured servitude was a common eighteenth-century practice and can perhaps be thought of as limited slavery. Once bonded, the servant and his labor, legally and literally, belonged to the master for the duration. For adults, this was usually seven years; for a child, like Carl Otto, his 14 years was common. Many German immigrants arrived as indentured servants, having sold their services to pay for their passage. While family tradition holds that Carl was "bound . . . to earn some of the money his father had to pay to bring the family across the ocean," his indenture, no doubt, actually provided his parents with a stake to establish themselves in farming, first in Berks County.

As with many ordinary German families, their early history is sketchy. The Revolutionary War brings them a bit more into focus. Peter served the Patriot cause, first in Captain Jacob Ladich's Company in Colonel Ely's Battalion of the Berks County Militia. He apparently later joined the 1st Battalion, Northampton County Militia in 1785 under the command of Lieutenant Colonel Michael Brobst. Tradition suggests that Peter's brother Carl also served in the Revolution, but no records verify this.

The role of the Germans in the American Revolution is little known, in a positive sense. "German" and "Revolution" to many means "the Hessians," the mercenaries George III hired from the Landgrave of Hesse to fight against the Revolutionaries. Few realize that many Hessians captured in the colonies were bound out, as was the custom at the time, as laborers or craftsmen to local merchants and farmers. There were no Prisoner of War camps. In Pennsylvania, many Hessians ended up bound to German speakers like themselves. A craftsman-Hessian, bound to the Kershner family of Lehigh County, did elaborate baroque plaster ceilings now in the Winterthur Museum. Many Hessian soldiers married into the families of their masters. At the end of the Revolution, a number of others preferred to remain in America where they could find better future prospects than in Germany. Many of the Dutch of eastern Pennsylvania, especially, have some Hessian in their ancestry.

The most renowned German celebrity of the Revolution is, of course, Prussian-born Baron von Steuben. von Steuben (1730–1794) came to America in 1777 and joined the Army the next year. Working closely with Washington, he remained in the Army until 1784 when Congress, as an act of gratitude, bestowed American citizenship upon him. He never returned to Germany, but spent the rest of his life in America, eventually dying in New York City. Frederich Willhelm Augustus von Steuben Day, celebrated annually in October, however, is no major event among the Dutch; rather, it has been celebrated by descendants of later immigrants to demonstrate their patriotism and loyalty.

While the important Battle of Germantown was fought near Philadelphia, and that city itself was occupied by British troops, much of the Dutch heartland went peacefully on its way during the Revolution, although like Peter Steigerwalt, many Dutch men and boys served in the Revolution. The graveyards of most early churches in the region contain graves of veterans of the Revolution, often proudly decorated with small American flags by local chapters of the Daughters of the American Revolution. Many of Peter's descendants are members.

As the years passed after the Revolution, the next generation of Steigerwalts established themselves as successful small farmers near the present town of Andreas in what was then Northampton County. The ancestral homes Peter, Carl, and Andrew built for their families, first of log, were replaced by substantial stone residences and some are still owned by their lineal descendants. All three brothers were active in the Ben Salem Lutheran Church in Ashfield (near Andreas) where many of the family remain members today. Other descendants are buried or own burial plots in the Ben Salem graveyard.

The picture that emerges of the family over the years is of people with large families who remained close to home. Most were farmers and/or craftsmen. Daughters married other farmers or craftsmen. The records note weavers, blacksmiths, lumbermen, teamsters, store keepers, tavern owners, teachers, and occasional ministers. Former indentured servant Carl's son, Frederick, stayed on the family homestead and married Maria Hettler. The couple produced twelve children: five sons and seven daughters—all of whom grew to maturity. Their valley must have been a healthy location and their genes sound because it is interesting to note how many large families lived to grow up.

Frederick and Maria's son, Charles, was quite the entrepreneur. He became a teamster, as related in Pansy Steigerwalt's *The Steigerwalt Family 1767–1979*:

> About that time he built a dam across the Lizard Creek south of his home. He built a saw mill, and the second son, Reuben, became the saw miller. He made his timber into boat luber [sic] which was hauled to Weissport. The lumber was hauled to the top of Mahoning Mountain by a team of four horses and taken the rest of the way by a team of two. A few years later he built a cider press; the builder was John Dieter Heintzelman, an expert woodworker.
>
> People who wanted cider had to make it themselves at this press and were customarily allowed two days for it. They generally cooked apple-butter at the same time, using a 32-gallon copper kettle and a "patented" ladle, ad [sic] contrivance with four blades which kept the apple-butter from sticking to the bottom of the kettle and burning. The cost for using the press was 6c for a barrel of cider and 25c for the use of the kettle.
>
> The oldest son became a weaver, and as the younger sons grew up they became teamsters. The father saw to it that each one had something to do. He had a flock of sheep, using the wool for clothing and the mutton for food. He also raised flax for clothing which the women made during the winter months.

The next major event to bring the clan into historic focus was the Civil War. We learn that during the hostilities, Charles's eldest son, also named Charles, "was living in Tamaqua and was drafted into the service. Levi, the younger brother, was also drafted, but since he [already] had a family, his younger brother Stephen took his place," according to *The Steigerwalt Family 1767–1979*. Among the most vividly remembered of the Steigerwalt Civil War veterans was Daniel Kressley (whose mother was a Steigerwalt descendant), who survived the bloodbath that is remembered as the Battle of Antietam. Returning to his ancestral region, he married and had a large family, including a daughter, Esther Suzanna, who was born in the Lizard Creek Valley in 1885 and married local farmer and woodcutter Franklin Steigerwalt. "Mama," as she became known to generations in the Valley, lived in her ancestral region until her death in 1983. She exemplified the basic conservatism of many of the Pennsylvania Dutch. She never had traveled more than 50 miles from her home and, although the railroad transversed her farm, she had never been on a train. All her long life, English was clearly her second language. As she aged, and long before her death, she spoke English only when she absolutely had to do so.

Even from the earliest days of settlement, however, there were others who could not wait to leave the valley—some drawn by the prospect of adventure, others by the promise of cheaper land, and yet others by the quest for higher education. Indeed, tradition holds that one of Johann Frederich's sons "migrated west" shortly after the family settled in the Lizard Creek Valley. Later genealogical work traced the adventurous soul to Indiana, where his descendants still live. World Wars I and II also took many Steigerwalt men out of the valley, and while they saw the world, most returned home, as did many of the Steigerwalt men who had worked for the railroad companies of their day.

When you look through the various volumes of Steigerwalt genealogies, you are struck by the sparsity of surnames before World War II. They reflect a society that was very traditional and devoutly Lutheran.

Typical of the transitional families within the Steigerwalt clan are Eugene Oscar Steigerwalt and Florence Caroline Steigerwalt, who were married in 1936. Both came from large families and both were educated pioneers in their families. Florence was the first girl in her valley to graduate from high school and she went on to college, graduating from Kutztown Normal School (now Kutztown University) as a teacher. Eugene worked his way through

Muhlenburg College and the Lutheran Theological Seminary in Philadelphia as a butcher. He was ordained in 1933. Interestingly, he commuted from Lehighton to Allentown and later to Philadelphia by trolley car—an inter-urban system destroyed by the automobile. As mentioned earlier, both came from large families and most of their siblings stayed in the region or returned back home.

The Steigerwalts had five children, and as they came of college age, the minister and the teacher, facing overwhelming college expenses, moved to California where tuition was free and where Florence earned an M.S. in Library Science from UCLA. As retirement approached for the Reverend Steigerwalt, the family, with one college child in tow, returned to Pennsylvania where Florence became government documents librarian in Harrisburg and the Reverend Steigerwalt became pastor of two Lutheran churches—one in Port Royal and the other in the tiny crossroads town of Nook, both in Juniata County.

Just one of their children, their only son, John, married Dutch—a daughter of a Lutheran minister who had been the proverbial "girl next door." For many years, the Steigerwalts had lived in Selinsgrove, which was a two–Lutheran church town. Pastor Steigerwalt's church was on one side of the street, and Pastor Turnbach's church was across the street. The two churches existed because of a doctrinal schism in the nineteenth century. In the second half of the twentieth century there was a healing when both congregations came together, demolished their old buildings, and constructed a new Colonial Revival sanctuary. Unfortunately, the union between John Steigerwalt and Susan Turnbach took an opposite turn: they were eventually divorced.

The four daughters married men of varied ancestries: Holland Dutch, Mexican, Italian-Swedish, and Jewish. John's second wife is of mixed ancestry, including Greek. The Steigerwalt genealogies all show these changes, as do family get-togethers.

Many of the hundreds of descendants of Ambrose and Alvesta Steigerwalt gathered at Fourth of July and Labor Day picnics at Lochner's Grove in Carbon County. Most lived nearby; many traveled to be with their kin. Even today, Dutch country is dotted with these groves—some privately owned, others owned by towns.

A Dutch Family

Lochner's Grove, now closed, was located down a dirt road off Route 895 in Andreas. It was primitive. Toilets were outhouses, but in a nod to modernity there was electricity. The grove had several pavilions. The largest housed the card games (mostly pinochle) and the major food consumption area. Another covered a grill, where the elders grilled frankfurters and hamburgers all day. The third housed barrels of beer for adults and root beer for children. Best of all, from the kids' point of view, there was also an old freezer stocked with tubs of ice cream and topped with boxes of cones and scoops. There were amusements: horseshoes and quoits, and large multi-generational baseball games. This was a time to visit, to gossip, and to eat and eat. Cousins, aunts, and uncles as far as the eye could see.

The elders' grill supplied snacks all day, not serious food. At about noon, real eating began, as each family carefully emptied the contents of their baskets and coolers onto the table. A veritable catalog of Dutch dishes emerged: sausage, ham, chicken, baked beans, three bean salad, coleslaw, potato salad, Chow-Chow, pickles (sweet and sour), pickled eggs, deviled eggs, and the homemade pastries—pies, cakes, and cookies.

Family culture dictated that families sat together with their food in front of them and that any picnicker was expected to walk along the tables and lean over and help themselves. In the 1980s, as the older generation died off, the picnics declined, and so did the quality of the food. More and more store-bought food arrived—supermarket platters of meats and cheese, cakes, and salads. Since no one was about to compliment you on your supermarket purchase, meals became buffet style—the dishes often interchangeable and anonymous. In the early 1990s, Lochner's Grove closed and a coup de grace was given to a waning picnic. Other Steigerwalt picnics, however, still go on. The Steigerwalt Family Reunion held its 95th edition on July 26, 2003, "Rain or Shine" at Zion's Grove.

In the 2003 newsletter, Anita Steigerwald Bond (vice president of the family reunion) reflects on the passage of time:

> Just as parties come and parties go, Reunions come and Reunions
> go, so too do the generations of the Steigerwalt family. What can you
> recall of the Civil War generation in your family? I am sure it isn't

much. A few good stories handed down through the generations. Whatever is documented about that generation is all that we have to remember them by. We didn't have the opportunity to meet them, or to ask the questions we had about their time in history. The WWI generation was my grandparents time in history, the time of the roaring 20's. WWII was my parents generation, the Big Band era. My era was the time of the VietNam war, Janis Joplin, The Beatles, and the "Flower Children." Our youth of today will remember their time in history as the time of the Gulf War and after September 11, 2001 another generation, and another war to remember. Isn't it strange how we seem to remember history by the tragedy of wars, and of the music of the time.

Chapter Six

THE PUBLIC DUTCH

Historically, the public life of the Dutch church people, or sectarians, revolved around their religious institutions and their religion-related institutions. Church buildings, or meetinghouses, are the most obvious structures, but so too are social welfare and educational institutions. In an age before Social Security and the many public services available to the indigent, orphanages were a fact of American life, and many of the Dutch provided religious-based institutions to deal with the unfortunates. Many of these still exist, although most have changed their focus. For example, The George Frey Orphans Home in Middletown, Dauphin County, founded in the nineteenth century, became Frey Village in the late twentieth century, serving the needs of senior citizens.

The relationship to education among the Dutch has long been complex. Because of their strong ethnocentric religious beliefs, most Dutch were very devoted to the concept of parochial schools, as the Amish and some Mennonites remain today. When Pennsylvania finally passed a Free Public School law in the first half of the nineteenth century, the greatest threat to its enforcement (as to its enactment) were many Germans who, rightly, believed that public education provided in English would impact unfavorably on the preservation of their culture. Assimilationists throughout Dutch country felt differently, and there were already many German-oriented schools. Run by the Moravians, the first group to believe in educating girls, Linden Hall Academy in Lititz, for example, was founded in the eighteenth century and remains a fine independent school for girls today. Many towns have old academy buildings, often now converted into apartments, that are remnants of an earlier educational system. Ephrata Academy, on the grounds of the Ephrata Cloister, is a rare intact survivor of the pre-public school era.

The Dutch attitude toward higher education was also conflicted, yet the need among the Lutherans, Evangelical Reformed Churches, and the

THE PENNSYLVANIA DUTCH COUNTRY

Moravians for a learned clergy was an important early impetus towards founding colleges. Dutch country is dotted with small independent liberal arts colleges whose roots are grounded in traditional religious beliefs. Some names are clearly Germanic: Muhlenberg, Albright, and Moravian. Others have geographic names, like Juniata, Susquehanna, or Lebanon Valley. The names of some reflect a desire to join the mainstream. Two small assimilationist colleges joined to form Franklin and Marshall College in Lancaster—today probably the most prestigious of the German-founded schools. Named after United States Supreme Court Justice John Marshall and Benjamin Franklin, the college is now secular.

The sectarians founded Elizabethtown College, home to "The Center for Anabaptist Studies." Two theological seminaries are located in Dutch country as well: Lutheran Theological Seminary in Gettysburg and Lancaster Theological Seminary in Lancaster City. Located across the street from Franklin and Marshall College, the seminary was founded to educate those no longer being served by the increasingly secular older school. Much newer is the Evangelical School of Theology, founded in 1953, in Myerstown, Lebanon County, and housed on a campus that had been the site of Albright (then Palatinate) College before it moved to Reading. The Evangelical School's primary purpose is to supply ministers for the Evangelical Congregational Church, a 30,000-member German-based group, but its course offerings are more far reaching.

Reflecting, and in fact leading many trends in Pennsylvania public life was the remarkable Muhlenberg family. The family founder in America was Henry Melchior Mühlenberg (1711–1787). Born in Hanover in Germany and university trained, he was ordained in the Lutheran church in Leipzig in 1739. Two years later he received a call to the United Congregations (Philadelphia, New Providence, New Hanover) in Pennsylvania. Landing in South Carolina, he traveled on to Philadelphia, arriving in November 1742. According to the *Dictionary of American Biography*, "He saw his task, almost from the beginning, not as serving of three isolated congregations but as the planting of a church, and to that great enterprise he brought talents of the highest order." By the time of this death, he was hailed as the "Patriarch of the Lutheran Church in America." He is buried beside the Augustus Church at Trappe (New Providence), which he had built years before.

Henry Melchior's family was equally remarkable. In 1745 he married Anna Maria Weiser, a daughter of Johann Conrad Weiser (1696–1760), one of the Penn family's chief Indian negotiators and one of the richest men in the Dutch countryside. Anna Maria bore six sons and five daughters. Three of these sons—Frederick Augustus (1750–1801), John Peter Gabriel (1746–1807), and Gotthilf Henry Ernest (1753–1815)—have had such great significance that they are listed in the Dictionary of American Biography.

The most celebrated in his own time was John Peter Gabriel, "The Fighting Parson" of Revolutionary War renown. Born in Trappe, he was the eldest of the 11 Muhlenberg children. Like his brothers, he was sent to study in Halle in Germany. Returning, he assisted his father, and then in 1771 he was called to a German Lutheran congregation at Woodstock, Virginia, but "in order to secure the priviledges [sic] of a clergyman" in Virginia's Established Church, he went to England and was ordained by the Bishop of London as an Episcopalian. Apparently he was never ordained as a Lutheran, although he only served Lutheran congregations. Drawn to politics, he was elected to the Virginia House of Burgess in 1774. A patriot, he "raised and commanded" Virginia's 8th Regiment, which was made up mostly of Shenandoah Valley Germans. On February 21, 1771, as a result of his leadership at the Battle of Sullivan's Island, he was commissioned a brigadier general in the Continental Army. Ordered north, he took part in the battles of Germantown and Monmouth Courthouse. He spent the famed winter with Washington and the troops at Valley Forge. Active in the Yorktown campaign that ended the Revolution, he was breveted a major general afterwards. To the Dutch of Pennsylvania he was a hero, second only to Washington, and he had a very successful political career after the war, including two terms in Congress and was elected to the U.S. Senate in 1801, but resigned to become supervisor of revenue for Philadelphia. Always proud of his heritage, he was president of the German Society of Pennsylvania from 1801 until his death in 1807.

His younger brother Frederick Augustus Conrad Muhlenberg (1750–1801) was ordained a Lutheran minister by the Ministerium of Pennsylvania at Reading in 1770. His religious career was short, however, and in 1779 he was elected and re-elected to the Continental Congress, and in 1787 he presided over the convention called to ratify the Federal Constitution. The next year he was elected to the First Congress as a Federalist from Philadelphia and served as speaker of the House for several years. Also a businessman, he employed his sugar refiner father-in-law's connections and was active as both a sugar refiner and an importer. Extremely fat, Frederick Augustus died from a stroke as a relatively young man.

The leading scholar among the brothers was Gotthilf Henry Ernest Muhlenberg (1753–1815), a precocious lad who was ordained at the age of 17. After service in Philadelphia and New Jersey, he was called to the Holy Trinity Lutheran Church in Lancaster, where he remained as pastor for 35 years. Additionally, in 1787, he became the first president of Franklin College (which would later join with Reformed Marshall College to form present-day Franklin and Marshall College).

Although his theological and educational careers were long, his major importance to American culture is as a pioneer botanist. Forced to return to Trappe when the British occupied Philadelphia, he lived in his father's house and turned to the study of botany. Corresponding with leaders in Europe, he was elected to several learned societies. Later, whenever his other duties allowed, he did field work and kept a calendar of flowering plants in his region. By 1791, he had listed over 1,100 plants growing within 3 miles of Lancaster. He always described the plants with precision. Among his many works was *A Catalogue of the Hitherto Known Native and Naturalized Plants of North America, Arranged According to the Sexual System of Linnaeus*, which was published in Lancaster in 1813.

The brothers and their siblings all had large families, and the daughters married into other notable families. Various descendants also distinguished themselves. Henry Augustus Philip Muhlenberg (1782–1844) was the third of Gotthilf Henry's eight children. Ordained a Lutheran minister in 1804, the next year he married Mary Elizabeth Hiester, whose father would later be governor of Pennsylvania.

Politics was in Henry Augustus's blood, and taking advantage of the prestige of his family name among the Dutch, he was elected to Congress from Berks County in 1829. Re-elected, he served until 1838, when he was named the first American minister to Austria. Unable to afford to remain a diplomat, he returned to America and in 1844 was in the midst of his campaign for governor of Pennsylvania when he died of a stroke.

Gotthilf's grandson Frederick Augustus Muhlenberg (1818–1901) was the son of a Lancaster banker and physician. Ordained a minister, he became a noted scholar of Greek. As a professor or president, he served five colleges in Pennsylvania. He was a professor at Franklin College from 1840 to 1850 and a leader in the movement for its union with Marshall College. Next, he became a professor at another Lutheran school, Pennsylvania College (now Gettysburg College) and was there at the time of the battle. "During the Gettysburg Campaign his house was pierced by a shell and pillaged by marauding soldiers," according to the *Dictionary of American Biography*. In 1867, he moved to Allentown to become the first president of Muhlenberg College, named in honor of his great-grandfather. Poorly funded, the school struggled during its early years, but was firmly established when he left to become president of Thiel College in Greenville, which he re-organized before his retirement in 1893 at age 75. He returned to his heartland and died in Reading. Like many in the less celebrated Steigerwalt clan, he married a cousin, Catherine Anna, daughter of Major Peter Muhlenberg, himself a grandson of John Peter Gabriel Muhlenberg.

The Wüster family is descended from two brothers born near Heidelberg in Germany who emigrated to America in the eighteenth century—one Anglicized his name to Wistar, one to Wister—and in true German fashion, some family members intermarried, creating the Wister-Wistars. Caspar Wistar (1696–1752) was a German-born glass maker who emigrated to America in 1717 and became a Quaker. In 1740, he purchased a large tract of land in Salem County, New Jersey, where he established a glasshouse, which under him and his son Richard lasted until 1791. While their livelihood was in New Jersey, the Wistars always considered Pennsylvania, and especially Philadelphia, their home. Unlike the Muhlenbergs, they early married out of their faith and kinship and quickly became less identified with the German culture. One of Wistar's grandsons, also a Caspar Wistar (1761–1818), was a physician educated in Philadelphia, then in London and Edinburgh. In 1808, he became professor of anatomy at the University of Pennsylvania and in 1811 published the first textbook on anatomy printed in America, *System of Anatomy*. Very involved in the social and scientific world of Philadelphia, in 1818 the botanist Thomas Nuttall named the splendid vine "Wisteria" for him.

THE PENNSYLVANIA DUTCH COUNTRY

On Wistar's death, his large anatomical collection was left to the University of Pennsylvania. Today, it is housed at the Wistar Institute of Anatomy and Biology at the university, which was founded, and well endowed, by Wistar's great grand-nephew Isaac Jones Wistar.

The Wister branch has been more literary than scientific. Sarah Wister (1761–1804) was a celebrated diarist who began a diary in 1777 that provides an important window into the colonial past. A kinsman, Owen Wister (1860–1938), was born in Germantown and went to Germantown Academy. His by then wealthy family sent him to St. Pauls School in Concord, New Hampshire, and then on to Harvard. Always sickly, in the 1880s he followed the example of his Harvard friend Theodore Roosevelt and went to the West to recuperate. He spent five summers near Buffalo, Wyoming, and turned his attention to writing about the West. His masterpiece was *The Virginian*, published in 1902. Immensely successful, by the year of his death (1938), it had sold over 1,500,000 copies. Fittingly, as a memorial, a peak in the Tetons was named after him. In good Dutch fashion, he had married Mary Channing Wister, a cousin, and he spent most of his life in Pennsylvania.

From a very early period, as attested to by the Muhlenbergs, the Dutch have been active politically. Under the Constitution of 1790, Pennsylvania's first democratic state constitution, five of the seven governors were Dutch and from the heartland. The first of these was Simon Snyder (1759–1819), born in Lancaster to Palatine immigrants. Apprenticed as a child, Simon was a tanner and a currier. About 1784, he moved to Selinsgrove in Northumberland (now Snyder) County where he opened a general store and entered politics. He served in the Pennsylvania Assembly from 1797 to 1807, with three terms as speaker. He was "a leader of the back-country democracy, [who] fought to liberalize the judiciary laws and to diminish the governor's powers." A Jeffersonian Republican, Snyder was elected governor in 1808 and re-elected by "overwhelming majorities" in 1811 and again in 1813. He was strongly devoted to states rights and internal improvements. "Exceedingly plain in his ways, he emulated Jeffersonian simplicity and instead of delivering his message to the legislature in person sent it in writing," according to the *Dictionary of American Biography*.

The Public Dutch

Joseph Hiester (1752–1832), who served as governor from 1820–1823, was the son of a Westphalian-born father who settled in Berks County where he and his two brothers bought a large tract of land and where Joseph was born. Raised a farm boy, he went to work for a prosperous Reading merchant, Adam Witman. Following in the best Horatio Alger tradition, he married the boss's daughter, Elizabeth, in 1771. An ardent patriot, he raised a company of Berks County soldiers in 1776 when under 25 years of age and was able to "furnish equipment and necessary funds for the march to join Washington's Army." Chosen "captain" of his troops, he was captured by the British during the Battle of Long Island and confined, for awhile, on the notorious prison ship *Jersey* before he was paroled and later repatriated. Promoted in 1777 to lieutenant colonel, he next saw service at Germantown where he received a minor wound.

After the war, politics called Hiester. From 1780 to 1790, he served in the Pennsylvania Assembly and was a member of the state convention called to ratify the Federal Constitution. He was, alas, one of the minority who opposed ratification. Elected to Congress, first in 1797, Thomas Jefferson considered him a "disinterested, moderate and conscientious . . . congressman. His tenure as governor largely uneventful." Adhering to his belief in the one-term principle, he declined running again and retired to his extensive business interests. He died a rich man, leaving an estate of $460,000.

George Wolf (1777–1840) was the son of an Alsatian-born father who had emigrated in 1751. Receiving his formal education at a local classic academy near his Northampton County birthplace, he read law in the office of John Ross, an Easton lawyer and a future state supreme court justice. Admitted to the bar at age 21, he opened his own very successful office in Easton and soon married Mary Erb, with whom he had nine children. Politics became his main interest. After serving in Congress, he was elected governor in 1829 and again in 1832. His years in office were tumultuous and party controversy lost him his bid for re-election in 1835. Despite his having been brought up in the Dutch belt, he early became an advocate of free public schools and his most enduring achievement was the passage, in 1834, of the Free School Act. Opposition was intense, but he prevailed. He ended his days in a profitable public position as collector of customs of the Port of Philadelphia.

His successor as governor, Joseph Ritner (1780–1869), became chief executive on a fluke, running as an anti-Masonic candidate against a now fractured Democratic Party that George Wolf could not control. Born in Berks County, Ritner's father was "a German emigrant and ardent Revolutionary patriot," according to the *Dictionary of American Biography*. Poorly educated but ambitious, George moved to the frontier town of Washington in western Pennsylvania where he developed a successful farm.

In the War of 1812 Ritner was a private. In his home community he became supervisor of roads, in building which he introduced the plow, and he also participated in numerous Democratic caucuses. His thrifty habit of hauling freight and driving stock to Philadelphia in slack seasons made this stout countryman, with his massive head, strong face, and broad chest, a familiar sight along main-traveled roads; and his extensive family connections made him favorably known in ten German counties. During service to the Assembly, 1821–1826, the speakership came to him twice, in 1825 and 1826, unanimously the second time.

His aversion to privilege and secret societies turned him into an anti-Masonic. Once elected, he was in the midst of a maelstrom. Constantly berated by the press, he had to deal with financial panic, rabid canal and railroad lobbyists, and anti-abolitionist rioting. He lost many of his battles, but with George Wolf he shared a commitment to public education and was able to obtain a large increase in the permanent school appropriation—and to enlarge the number of public schools in Pennsylvania. After his term ended, he became a Whig and then a Republican. His last public office was as inspector of Pennsylvania's public schools.

Pennsylvania would have two new constitutions in the nineteenth century—one in 1838 and another in 1874, which lasted until 1968. Of the nine governors who served under the constitution of 1838, at least five—David Rittenhouse Porter, Francis Rawn Shunk, William Bigler, James Pollack, and John Frederick Hartranft—were of Dutch ancestry. Most interesting of these was Hartranft (1830–1889), who had been born near Fagleysville in Montgomery County. Attending Marshall and Union Colleges, he was trained as a civil engineer, but switched to law and politics. When the Civil War broke out, he enlisted in the Montgomery County Militia, which became the 4th Pennsylvania Regiment. Rising quickly through the ranks, by war's end Hartranft was a major general. His most significant battle was at Spotsylvania Courthouse.

A staunch Republican, as were many northern military heros, Hartranft was elected governor in 1872 and would serve two terms—once under the Constitution of 1838 and again under the Constitution of 1874, which he had helped craft. During his years as governor, 1873–1879, Pennsylvania industry expanded, but it also went through a period of intense labor unrest beginning with the Panic of 1876. According to the *Dictionary of American Biography*:

> By 1877, disturbances bordering on civil war existed in various parts of the state, especially in Philadelphia and Reading. The governor made frequent use of the state militia and . . . called on the federal government for soldiers, taking personal charge of the troops.

In a more glorious vein, he helped promote the Philadelphia Centennial Exposition (World Fair) in 1876. Highly respected in his time, an equestrian statue of him was erected on the Capitol grounds after his death. Like many of his predecessors, his last public office was as collector of the Port of Philadelphia (1881–1885), where presumably he could legally line his pockets.

The governors under the constitution of 1874 came from more varied backgrounds than their predecessors, although at least 7 of the 25 had Dutch or German ancestry. The most recent of these were George Michael Leader, who served from 1955–1959, whose ancestry was deeply rooted in York County; and Raymond P. Shafer (1967–1971), whose family was settled in Erie County. Two governors, Samuel Whitaker Pennypacker and Martin Grove Brumbaugh, were especially important because of their devotion to their Dutch heritage.

Martin Grove Brumbaugh (1862–1930) was the son of German Baptist or Dunker parents. Born in Huntington County, he was extremely well educated and represented a whole new generation of the more cosmopolitan Dutch. After graduating from Juniata College, he went on to do graduate work at Harvard and the University of Pennsylvania, earning a Ph.D. in 1894. A Republican, his career nevertheless bears a resemblance to that of Democrat

Woodrow Wilson, a contemporary whose career in academia also led to a career in politics. Whereas Wilson used the governorship of New Jersey as a springboard to the Presidency, Brumbaugh's governorship, 1915–1919, was the end of his public life. A staunch laissez-faire conservative, he vetoed over 400 bills during his administration, although he did allow several measures that dealt with child welfare and workman's compensation to become law. As governor when World War I broke out, Brumbaugh organized the Council of Defense, whose task it was to coordinate the commonwealth's war effort.

An educator by profession who became president of Juniata College, Brumbaugh was actively interested in his heritage and was a member of the Historical Society of Pennsylvania and the Pennsylvania German Society. He was the author of *A History of the Germanic Baptist Brethren in Europe and America*, published in 1899. His son G. Edwin Brumbaugh became a pioneer architect specializing in historic preservation. Among the important sites he restored is the incomparable Ephrata Cloister in Lancaster County and the Daniel Boone Homestead in Berks County.

Governor Brumbaugh's predecessor, who served as the commonwealth's chief executive from 1903–1907, Samuel Whitaker Pennypacker, was a Republican in the mode of President Theodore Roosevelt. Both were honest, progressive, and scholarly. Both were descended from very early American stock. Born in Phoenixville, Pennypacker was the descendant of Heinrich Pannebäcker, who arrived in Pennsylvania before 1699. A graduate of the University of Pennsylvania, he became a lawyer and then a judge. As governor, he was honest, creative, and effective. He forced through a long delayed, constitutionally mandated re-apportionment of the state legislature, curbed corrupt electoral practices, and established the Department of Health. He paid down the state debt and left a large balance in the treasury even after the cost of the new state capitol, the construction of which was mired with graft. Never suspected while in office, later investigations proved the governor to have been innocent of any wrongdoing. He and President Theodore Roosevelt dedicated the great new Renaissance Style building.

As governor, Pennypacker was a strong supporter of the conservation of forest lands and historic sites. His serious historical interests began about 1872 when he joined the Historical Society of Pennsylvania, which he would serve as president from 1900–1916. He collected an unrivaled 10,000 books and documents pertaining to Pennsylvania history and was a pioneer collector of Pennsylvania Dutch stuff. He bought a country farm with family associations, "Pennypacker Mills," near Schwenksville in Montgomery County, where he housed most of his collections and gloried in his heritage. The house is today a museum whose exterior walls are in places decorated with tiles in honor of the distant ancestor (Pannebäcker means "tile baker"). The numerous Pennypacker-Pennybaker clan now holds occasional reunions at the homestead.

Of the six governors under the new twentieth-century constitution of 1968, only one, Mark Schweiker of Bucks County, is of Dutch ancestry. Elected as lieutenant governor, he became governor when Tom Ridge was tapped by President George W. Bush to head national security efforts after September 11, 2001.

The story of Pennsylvania and politics and public services continues. Many local officials are Dutch, as are members of the judiciary and the legislature. There are many others who are the product of intermarriage who may bear English, Polish, or Italian names who are also very proud of their Dutch roots. State Senator Joe Conti of Bucks County is one of those who fondly remembers his traditional Dutch grandmother, and he regards pork and sauerkraut as soul food, right along with lasagna.

Chapter Seven

POPULAR IMAGES OF THE DUTCH

There is an ever-increasing number of scholarly books being published about the Pennsylvania Dutch, including annual volumes published under the auspices of the Pennsylvania German Society, which was founded in 1891 in the post–Civil War era, which saw the emergence of many philo-patristic organizations that celebrated the glories of pre-Revolutionary ancestry. Most famous of these are the Daughters of the American Revolution and the Society of Mayflower Descendants, where applicants must prove their ancestry. Today, the Pennsylvania German Society, housed in Kutztown, is open to anyone interested in the culture, no questions asked—just pay your dues (currently $55 a year and up). Members receive the Society's annual publication, which for the past several years has been published in cooperation with the Pennsylvania State University Press. The most recent annual volume, the 2002 book, is Jeff Bach's *Voices of the Turtledoves*, which is a detailed, scholarly study that historian Donald F. Durnbaugh notes, "offers the first satisfying explanation of the Ephrata Cloister," and while "there have been scores of books and hundreds of articles attempting to portray this fascinating yet mystifying religious complex . . . none has [before] succeeded in uncovering the basic ideology and motivation of its founder Conrad Beissel and its several hundred members."

Among the Society's other recent publications have been books on church pewter, fraktur, and sectarian women's lives—all of which stand in contrast to the broad themes of the early years of the twentieth century with titles like *Pennsylvania Germans in the Revolutionary War*. Many of these books were, and continue to be, written by Pennsylvania Dutch authors. Most have had small and often parochial circulation.

Works of fiction, along with movies and television shows about the Dutch, have been much rarer and they have especially dealt with the Amish and the Mennonites—very rarely with the normative Dutch.

THE PENNSYLVANIA DUTCH COUNTRY

The Pennsylvania Dutch have produced few major novelists themselves and perhaps the best depiction of them in popular fiction is in the work of a writer of Irish descent, John O'Hara (1905–1970), who was born in Pottsville, Schuylkill County, and grew up on fashionable Mahantango Street as the son of a prominent physician. A novelist whose career spanned the decades of the 1930s through the 1960s, O'Hara, the subject of a new biography, *The Art of Burning Bridges: A Life of John O'Hara*, by Geoffrey Wolff (2003), was extremely popular, with many of his books being made into motion pictures. The terrain that became O'Hara country centered on Schuylkill County, but also extended further, especially down to Harrisburg, the state capital. In later years, he turned the focus of his writing to New York and Hollywood.

O'Hara called Pottsville "Gibbsville," and Schuylkill County "Lantenengo County." In *Appointment in Samara*, published in 1934, the major characters all live on Lantenengo Street, the Mahantango Street of John O'Hara's youth. The elite of Gibbsville are Protestant. Wealthy Catholics are tolerated, and Jews—well, there were only the Brombergs and ". . . having the Brombergs on Lantenengo Street hurt real estate values. Everybody said so. The Brombergs . . . had paid thirty thousand for . . . [the house in which they lived] twelve thousand five hundred more than Will Price had been asking; but if the Brombergs wanted to live on Lantenengo Street, they could pay for it." The Protestant elite were of British Islands and Pennsylvania German ancestry and, indeed, the first of the characters we meet on a Christmas morning is an overhung Luther L. (L for LeRoy) Fliegler "who belonged on Lantenengo Street" and his wife Irma "whose family had been in Gibbsville a lot longer than the great majority of people who lived on Lantenengo Street." Shortly we meet Julian English, the tragic British Island–descended hero of the novel, and by book's end, we learn about the events that led to his downfall

The details of 1920s parties at the Lantenengo Country Club are precise, boozy, and naughty. The Dutch in this group are not the rather dour people who live "in the Pennsylvania Dutch part of the County" where cheating husbands from Gibbsville "thought they were getting away with murder by taking their girlfriends to the area's country hotels." In the Prohibition time of the novel, Gibbsville's smart set drank at home (thanks to a bootlegger), "at the Stage Coach, which was the big roadhouse, where drinks were six bits apiece and there was dancing and a hat-check girl," and of course at the country club.

In O'Hara's *Ten North Frederick*, published in 1955, the author returns to Gibbsville to introduce us to the very wealthy Chapin family and to the cultural side of Gibbsville where snobbery and pretense reigned. In these circles, it was best to be of British Islands descent, but the respectable Dutch were welcomed. Gibbsville Country Day was an important line of demarcation for those who really mattered:

> The original G.C.D. building was a converted mansion at 16th and Christiana, once the home of the Rutter family, of the Rutter Brewery. When Jacob Rutter built his house he bought a block of land, with a stand of trees, and he had what amounted to a private park within the borough limits of Gibbsville. The Rutter line died out with Jacob and for more than a year the house was not occupied, until the gentlemen who were organizing Gibbsville Academy, predecessor of G.C.D., bought the property. Half of the block was promptly sold for middle-class home sites, leaving adequate grounds for the school.

Note that the Rutter mansion was the home of a brewer who would probably have been a nineteenth-century arrival into the community, as was the real Yuengling family in the real Pottsville. Also note that O'Hara suggests that the school cut corners. It is difficult to imagine Buckley in New York City selling half its site for middle class homes. The school also made its compromises in its choice of headmaster, who was Pennsylvania Dutch.

Writing the forward to a new edition of *Appointment in Samara*, published in 1953, O'Hara discusses a point crucial to his depiction of the Dutch as well as the other characters in his Dutch country novels: "How much of this novel is true?" he asks rhetorically. "It's all true, a rather pompous remark that needs extending. . . . what I really mean when I say it's all true is that the psychological patterns were real. Just as in several other novels of mine (notably *A Rage to Live*) the quick reader thought he had identified my characters from real life, and he always guessed wrong."

THE PENNSYLVANIA DUTCH COUNTRY

Like many good writers, O'Hara was a keen observer and a careful listener. He was also a near outsider, being Catholic in a very Protestant world. Yet the sport of trying to identify "real" people in his books still goes on. People in Pottsville and Schuylkill County are ambivalent about O'Hara to this day, but in an area in economic and perhaps cultural decline they cannot easily dispose of one of their few real, enduring celebrities: a state historic marker was erected at his birthplace and many locals can show you where he grew up. To read his novels is to know the scene. Much of Mahantango Street is still grand or being restored.

No single O'Hara novel created the furor that *A Rage to Live* did. Set mostly in the Teens and Twenties, it was published in 1949 and prefaced with the following:

> . . . because this is a work of fiction I have had to obliterate Harrisburg and Dauphin and the Susquehanna and substitute Fort Penn and Nesquehela, county and river. I also have made a complete substitution of the population past and present of Harrisburg and Dauphin County, and anyone who thinks he sees himself or anyone else in this novel is wrong.

As with today's "Law and Order" disclaimer, no one believed him. *A Rage to Live* was widely excoriated and avidly read in Dauphin County, despite, or perhaps because the book was banned from the city's public library for many years. Today, everyone denies that this was the case.

During a lecture by O'Hara at the Dauphin County Historical Society in the early 1950s, when asked where he learned all the Harrisburg gossip that he incorporated into *A Rage to Live*, O'Hara simply answered, "From my mother!" "The audience," historian Don Kent recalled, "gasped."

The central characters of *A Rage to Live* are Grace Caldwell and Sidney Tate. She was the scion of a very wealthy and powerful local family, the most prominent family in Fort Penn, and he was the son of wealthy New Yorkers. His father had been born in England and his mother, we are told, is of "old New York stock." The Tates are rich, the Caldwells are richer. As a senior at Yale, Sidney decides that he wants to become a gentleman farmer and it is his love of farming that brings him to Dutch country searching for land. Sidney meets Grace through the accident that he and her brother, Brock, both went to Lawrenceville and Yale. Grace's family owns a magnificent farm among its many assets, and love blossoms.

As the novel opens, there is a festival being held July 4, 1917, to benefit the Red Cross at the Tate's Riverside Farm. The Tates are clearly the golden couple of Fort Penn. Their sponsorship ensures that everyone will be there, including "His Excellency the Hon. Karl F. Dunkelberger, Governor of the Commonwealth of Pennsylvania" who "returned greetings in English and in Pennsylvania Dutch." On the speaker's stand, "He pronounced did, dit; ever with a W instead of a V, ugly, uckly. He made himself deliberately Dutchy so that he would have the predominantly Dutch crowd with him."

Both Sidney and Grace have close friends who are Dutch and we are brought into their worlds as well. Grace's friend was Connie Schoffstal and Sidney's was Paul Reichelderfer. Both are delicious characters.

To find the farm of his dreams, Sidney contacts Reichelderfer, an old Yale friend and fellow member of the elite Death Heads Society. Paul, whose father was extremely Dutchy, bridges the two worlds interestingly.

> He was an amiable fat boy with a remarkable capacity for beer. He was so big that he had to go to a tailor for his clothes, but he did more than go to a tailor; he went to a good one. Like all fat men, he had to have money to eat, but he had more than enough for that; he was rich. Buried in the fat face was a thin handsome face, with a neat, rather sharp nose and small, alert blue eyes. He ate big, drank big, smoked big, and his frolics with women were prodigious. . . .

Sidney's visit was unsuccessful and he couldn't find a farm. Good farms, he learned, "usually stayed in the family."

But another reason for the visit was to have a good time—and this was a success as he was introduced to chicken and waffles and the full abundance of local food, followed by another and more surprising tradition, a farting exhibition. This is very much in line with the Dutch love of bathroom humor.

Through Grace Caldwell's friendship with Connie Schoffstal, O'Hara invites readers into the world of the extended kinship common among the

Germans. The area around Fort Penn was thick with Schoffstals, who all felt an obligation for one another's welfare:

> A candidate for county office who carried the entire Schoffstal vote would have had a head-start on almost any other candidate. There were Schoffstals in townships where there were no Schmidts or Hoffmans or Steins or Millers, and when a Miller or a Stein or a Hoffman or a Schmidt married a Schoffstal, he too became a Schoffstal. The Miller or Schmidt did not change his name; he didn't have to. It was known that he had married a Schoffstal, and a man's standing in his township or borough sometimes was determined by the closeness or remoteness of his kinship with the Fort Penn Schoffstals . . .

Along with kinship, religion mattered very much, with Lutheranism being preferred: "Any Schoffstal who came to Fort Penn, who was clean and neat and had a letter, preferably from the Lutheran pastor, was helped."

When *A Rage to Live* was made into a movie in 1965, perhaps not surprisingly, all the Pennsylvania Dutch aspects of the novel were deleted. The film, made in a Hollywood studio except for an opening establishment shot of Front Street in Harrisburg, concentrated on Sidney and Grace and especially her adulterous affair. Starring Suzanne Pleshette, Bradford Dillman, and Ben Gazarra, the film sank into well-deserved obscurity.

Arthur H. Lewis (*b.* 1906) was a newspaperman turned best-selling author of biographies and popular histories, including *Lament for the Molly Maguires*, which would be made into a major motion picture. His Pennsylvania Dutch bestseller, *Hex*, explores an incident in York County related in this recently-reprinted news story from the November 30, 1928, Lancaster *New Era*:

> FARMER SLAIN: Witchcraft was blamed for the brutal slaying of a 59 year old York County farmer who was beaten to death with clubs and a chair. Police said he was killed while resisting an attempt by three suspects, ages 14, 18, and 32, to obtain a lock of his hair. They had hoped to bury the hair underground in an effort to break a spell the victim allegedly had cast on the 18 year old's father.

The more superstitious of these often rural Dutch really embraced (or never abandoned) their pre-Christian heritage. Writing about one of the killer's family in *Hex*, Lewis observed:

> Technically speaking, the Blymires were Lutherans, but except for weddings and funerals they rarely attended services at St. John's, the small church which served local farmers of that Christian denomination. Even though a large family Bible was to be seen in the Blymire parlor and a half-dozen pictures of Christ adorned the walls, their true Holy Writ, as in hundreds of other Pennsylvania Dutch households, was John George Homan's *The Long Lost Friend.*

The whole sordid tale can perhaps be called the "Tale of the Two Pow-Wowers." The second was Nelson D. Rehmeyer, who was apparently much more successful at his craft than was poor, inept John H. Blymire. The story of the tragedy is, at heart, simple. A branch of the Hess family of York County fell on hard times and, believing they were bewitched, hired John Blymire to "try" for them. The Hesses and he eventually came to believe that it was Nelson Rehmeyer who was the culprit.

The family of Milton J. and Alice Ouida Hess were avid believers in hexeri and had faithfully done everything tradition demanded, obeying all the laws laid down by generations of brauchers. And for many years the family was blessed with a successful and abundant life. Then in the spring of 1927, the family's luck broke and they felt like they were being subjected to the trials of Job. "All at once," Hess testified, "my wheat and my corn was no good and my potatoes were rotten. My chickens was stole and what hens was left wouldn't lay. My cattle wouldn't eat and couldn't give no milk."

In addition to the agricultural difficulties, Lewis quotes Hess describing his physical ailments: "I felt as though, all of a sudden, my flesh was being boiled continuously," Hess lamented. "I couldn't work; I couldn't rest. I was in a terrible predicament, and that just kept me so wonderful that I just had at last to be convinced that there was somethin' doing . . ."

There was for Milton and Alice Ouida only one explanation for their reversals. "We was bewitched," Milton maintained. When Rehmeyer refused entreaties to lift the spell and, indeed, denied casting it, John Blymire, his 14-year-old apprentice John Curry, and 18-year-old Wilbert Hess went to Rehmeyer Hollow to get the man's copy of *The Good Friend* and a lock of his hair. Burying these, they believed, would break the spell. Armed with "fourteen lengths of heavy rope" they set off. They knew that Rehmeyer would resist but, at first, he was so sure of his powers and "perhaps even amused at the effrontery of a witch whose powers had long since waned" he made no resistance except to deny that he had "The Book." What followed was quick and brutal.

> "Blymire shouted out, 'Tie his legs, John, so we can cut his hair!'"
>
> . . . "But the old man kicked hard and the rope flew out of my hands and he knocked me away," the fourteen-year old conspirator said. "Then Rehmeyer yells out, 'Let me up and I'll give you the book.' So Hess and Blymire who're sittin' on him, let him up. He stands in the middle of the floor, reaches in his pants and throws his pocket-book at Blymire."
>
> "Blymire says, 'That's not the book I mean and you know it.' Then the old man goes for Blymire full force."
>
> After tossing his pocket-book at Blymire, who disregarded it, the older witch fought desperately, realizing for the first time that his life might be in danger despite his powerful physique and the quantities of Himmels-briefs he had on hand.
>
> "When Curry walks out to the wood box and gets a block and hits Rehmeyer over the head twict. We wuz beatin' him at the same time. Curry hits him again with the block and the blood just rushed out. Then Curry dropped the block and walked 'round him."

When it was over Blymire reportedly said, "Thank God! The witch is dead."

The trial, held in the York County Courthouse, was quick and a media circus. Reporters from all over the country converged on York and had a field day exposing the superstitious Pennsylvania Dutch as "hicks" and "backwoodsmen." On January 14, 1929, the men were sentenced: Blymire and Curry were given life sentences, and Hess "a term from ten to twenty years."

In 1953 the three men were paroled and they went on to lead quiet honest lives, with John Curry even becoming a local artist of note.

As gripping as the story of the witch killing was, Lewis's revelation that pow-wowing was still active in York County in 1969, for example, in the person of Mr. Ervin B. Emig of 1198 Prospect Street, was a sensation that made national headlines.

The story of *Hex* is a view into the dark side of a culture that often believed, and still to an extent believes, in the superstitions. Among these were:

> One should neither plant nor construct anything on Ascension Day; otherwise the crops will fail and the buildings burn or be struck by lightning. Vinegar barrels must be stirred on the first Friday before the new moon. A baby should be carried to the attic as soon after birth as possible so it will grow up with a "high mind."

Arthur H. Lewis also wrote a single novel, *The Copper Beeches*, which is a genial detective story whose villain was H. Wesley Eberhardt, "born April 17, 1918, in Lancaster, Pennsylvania, the second oldest of five siblings, three girls and two boys. His father, Kenneth H. Eberhardt, was an Evangelical Lutheran minister." As the book follows Eberhardt's trail throughout Central Pennsylvania, they have an especially Dutchy experience when they meet Mr. George ("Call me Chorch") Beebelheimer, the proprietor of Glen Hall, York County Funeral Home, and his muscular female assistant "Chosie" (Josie).

> "Chorch" is a short, fat Pennsylvania Dutchman, bald expect for tufts of pinkish hair which stuck out like miniature coxcombs on both sides of his large, otherwise bald head. His accent is incredible, at times so thick we had trouble translating it into English. At first, in writing this history, I attempted to phoneticize Mr. Beebelheimer's speech but . . . I soon gave up. With the exception of a few of the mortician's particularly choice words and phrases, I am permitting him to speak the English language after his peculiar fashion.

And Lewis's description of a transaction with the villain, who had arranged a funeral with "Chorch," is entertaining:

"The chentelman skims through the bill real fast like he doan give a damn. But then he comes to the last item and vhen he sees that he gets red in the face, sucks in his breath hard and stares at me like a crazy man."

"Honorarium for the breacher!" he perty near shouts. "Not one goddamned cent for no barson. Take that outa the bill or I'll call the whole thing off and have my friend cremated. If you want a breacher, then pay him yourself. I won't!"

While the church people, i.e., the Lutherans, especially, have appeared as supporting players in the popular works of O'Hara and Lewis, it is the Amish and the Mennonites who get top billing in the most popular books, movies, and television series. This is perhaps due to their relative exoticism; but as has been noted earlier, to many Americans, the Amish and the Mennonites *are* the Pennsylvania Dutch. Popular novels about the plain people began to be written in the late nineteenth century and became a cottage industry for three remarkable women: Helen Reimensnyder Martin (1868–1939), Phebe Gibbons (1821–1893), and Elsie Singmaster (1879–1958).

Of these, the most successful and famous was Helen Reimensnyder Martin, born to a Dutch family in Lancaster and educated at Swarthmore College and at Radcliffe. She is representative of three early twentieth-century movements. One is the emergence of the "new woman," a woman of letters, usually associated with the worlds of New England and New York, best characterized by Amy Lowell and Edith Wharton. Another is the world of regional literature, written by local authors, as exemplified by Joel Chandler Harris or S. Weir Mitchell. The third aspect is one that is very much localized among the Pennsylvania Dutch, characterized by the emergence of a highly educated class, as we have seen in Paul Reichelderfer in *A Rage to Live*.

Helen Reimensnyder Martin wrote about her changing world. Her books were many and included *Sabrina: A Story of the Amish* (1905), *Martha of the Mennonite Country* (1915), and *The Order of Minnie Schultz* (1939). But her best known book was *Tillie: A Mennonite Maid*, subtitled *A Story of the Pennsylvania Dutch*, published in 1904 and illustrated by pioneer female illustrator Florence Scovel Shinn. The Martin-Shinn volume went through 20 editions. Martin's novels are not very sentimental and she is much less sympathetic to the Mennonites than were Phebe Gibbons and Elsie Singmaster.

"Tillie," Matilda Maria Getz, the heroine, is a rebellious girl who prefers reading and learning to doing farm work or household chores. This is clearly an affront to her very gruff and traditional father Jacob Getz, who on several occasions beats her—and to her church, which castigates her. A marriage is arranged for her, but she refuses, and ultimately with the inspiration or guidance of teachers and a few other allies she triumphs. However, this is not an exposé nor is it a proto-feminist manifesto. It is, rather, a view of the world as it is and a statement of a belief in modernism.

It is not a dialect novel; patois is never used for its own sake. Dutchy patterns are only used to establish character. The novel's tone is beautifully set in the opening paragraph, when the child's happiest moment to date is to have fainted and been picked up by her teacher, the beautiful and tender Miss Margaret: ". . . it was in that blissful moment that Tillie had discovered, for the first time in her young existence, that life could be worth while. Not within her memory had any one ever caressed her before, or spoken to her tenderly, and in that fascinating tone of anxious concern."

Soon we learn that Miss Margaret isn't from around here; she's from Kentucky, and "not being a Millersville Normal [i.e. a graduate of Millersville Normal School in Lancaster County] she differed quite radically from any teacher they had ever had in New Canaan." The school itself wasn't a dream of the good old days, but rather, "This country school-house was a dingy little building in the heart of Lancaster County, the Home of the Pennsylvania Dutch." Martin's description of the Getz family is also far from the rosy ideal:

> Tillie's father was a frugal, honest, hard-working and very prosperous Pennsylvania Dutch farmer, who thought he religiously performed his parental duty in bringing up his many children in the fear of his heavy hand, in unceasing labor, and in almost total abstinence from all amusement and self-indulgence. Far from thinking himself cruel, he was convinced that the oftener and the more vigorously he applied "the strap," the more conscientious a parent was he.

His wife, Tillie's stepmother, was as submissive to his authority as were her five children and Tillie. Apathetic, anemic, overworked, she yet never dreamed of considering herself or her children abused, accepting her lot as the natural one of woman, who was created to be a child-bearer, and to keep men well fed and comfortable.

While the Getzs were well to do, the family had a shabby air about them. Tillie's family was not aberrant, but normative in the region, even if the father was perhaps considered too zealous:

> The Getz family was a perfectly familiar type among the German farming class of southeastern Pennsylvania. Jacob Getz, though spoken of in the neighborhood as being "wonderful near," which means very penurious, and considered by the more gentle-minded Amish and Mennonite of the township to be "overly strict" with his family and "too ready with the strap still," was nevertheless highly respected as one who worked hard and was prosperous, lived economically, honestly, and in the fear of the Lord, and was "laying by."

Tillie's home, like her family, was prosperous. It is interesting to note in the description of the farm the barn was behind the house rather than on axis as was, and is, more common.

> The Getz farm was typical of the better sort to be found in that county. A neat walk, bordered by clam shells, led from a wooden gate to the porch of a rather large, and severely plain frame house, facing the road. Every shutter on the front and sides of the building were tightly closed, and there was no sign of life about the place. A stranger, ignorant of the Pennsylvania Dutch custom of living in the kitchen and shutting off the "best rooms,"—to be used in their mustiness and stiff unhomelikeness on Sunday only,—would have thought the house temporarily empty. It was forbiddingly and uncompromisingly spick-and-span.

> A grass-plot, ornamented with a circular flower-bed, extended a
> short distance on either side of the house. But not too much land
> was put to such unproductive use; and the small lawn was closely
> bordered by a corn-field on the one side and on the other by an
> apple orchard. Beyond stretched the tobacco- and wheat-fields, and
> behind the house were the vegetable garden and the barn-yard.

There was a great deal of animosity directed at reading for pleasure in her family, especially by women, and Tillie, having been lent a book—a copy of *Ivanho* by Sir Walter Scott—had to sneak it into the house.

She continues her studies whenever and however she can, encouraged first by Miss Margaret, and then by William Fairchilds—an outsider—a Harvard graduate who has arrived from New England to help the benighted Dutch. Eventually she becomes a teacher, refuses to marry the man her father chooses for her, and risks losing her teaching certification. Rescued by Miss Margaret, now an instructor in English at Millersville Normal School as well as a married woman, Tillie goes to Europe to help her former teacher care for her children. She marries Fairchilds, now a professor at Millersville.

While *Tillie: A Mennonite Maid* is breathless and a bit precious in its writing, it is also filled with wonderful insights into the Dutch lifestyle—albeit, with some a bit generalized—to give the impression that common customs were universal customs.

Pennsylvania's normal schools, like those in other states, were designed to train teachers for the ever-growing school-age population. Aside from a few elite private schools like Bryn Mawr, they provided the only place a young woman could receive an education and become a professional. In Dutch country, there were two State Normal Schools—at Millersville in Lancaster County, and Kutztown in Lehigh County. Both would become colleges and then universities. But from their earliest incarnation, they were engines of change in Dutch country.

In 1974, James A. Michener, one of America's most renowned authors, published an amazing novel entitled *Centennial*, which traced the history of a fictional town, Centennial, Colorado, from the days when the earth was new. When it came to peopling the community, Michener traced their courses across America. One of his important characters was Levi Zendt, born and raised a Mennonite in Lancaster County. Of old stock, his ancestor Melchior Zendt had arrived from Germany in 1701 and the Zendts had thrived and grown prosperous as farmers and purveyors of prime meat products to the town of Lancaster. Why then did young Zendt leave all this in 1844? Because of an event that happened after market one night when Levi was taking leftover bits of meat to the local orphanage. Along for the ride was impetuous local girl Rebecca Stoltzfus, who falsely accuses him of attempted rape.

News of the event spread through Lancaster County. Eli was shunned and decided to leave and go to Colorado country. He bought a Conestoga wagon and six horses, a gun, and headed west, stopping first at the orphanage asking the orphan Elly Zahm to go with him—which she did.

Zendt's past life is stripped away as he travels west. Eventually he marries the Indian maiden Clay Basket after Elly dies of a rattlesnake bite. He shaves his beard, appears in Native American dress, and ceases to be a Pennsylvania Dutchman. He and his Indian wife were new Americans who would sire a race of newer Americans. The story is a compelling shorthand account of Americanization, but part of Michener's genius lay in his details. Before writing his books, he did extensive research into the region about which he wrote. His snapshots of Lancaster County in the 1840s are wonderfully rich. This area was viewed by many of the Dutch and their English counterparts as the American Eden:

> The Lancaster farmer did not exaggerate when he boasted, "On this land a good man can grow anything except nutmeg." And on all of it he could make a handsome profit, for his farm lay within marketing distance of Philadelphia and Baltimore. Corn, wheat, sorghum, hay, truck, tobacco and even flowers could be got to market, but it was the animals who prospered most and provided the best income, particularly cattle and hogs. Lancaster beef and pork were the standards of excellence against which others from less fortunate regions were judged.

Michener saw the local Mennonites in a brighter light than did Martin:

In most other parts of the world Mennonites would have seemed impossibly rigid, but when compared to the Amish they were downright frivolous, for they indulged in minor worldly pleasures, were expert in conducting business and allowed their children other choices than farming. Some Mennonite children even went to school. But when they did farm, they did it with vigor and were wonderfully skilled in extracting from their soil its maximum yield. When this was accomplished, they became uncanny in their ability to peddle it at maximum profit.

Centennial was a runaway best seller and was made into a thirteen-part mini-series that aired from October 1978 to February 4, 1979. The Lancaster County sequence predictably centered on Levi's entanglements and completely avoided the food-loving references. Adding insult to injury, the outdoor sequences were filmed in Ohio rather than Lancaster and lacked the air of truth that is often the case when the Dutch, and usually the Amish, are portrayed on the stage, in the movies, or on television.

Any book on the Pennsylvania Dutch should mention John Updike, who was born in Shillington in Berks County in 1932. Cynthia Ozick, writing in the *New York Times*, notes, "Updike is the most rootedly American (though German, not WASP stock) and the most self consciously Protestant" of America's contemporary fiction writers. Updike was a prodigy. After high school in Shillington, he attended Harvard and Oxford and from 1955 to 1957 he was on the staff of *The New Yorker*. His novels are studies of character with relatively little local color. His first major novel, *Rabbit, Run* (1960), however, is set in Central Pennsylvania. His hero—or anti-hero—is Rabbit Angstrom, who appears in two other Rabbit novels, as well. Later, Updike and his family moved to New England where he continues to live and write, but not about his native region. In *Rabbit, Run*, Rabbit drives to Lancaster and sees an Amish buggy, and his thoughts are bizarre. Updike is not so much describing the Amish as reacting to them through the eyes of his alienated young man:

Outside of Churchtown he passes an Amish buggy in the dark and catches a glimpse of a bearded man and a woman in black in this horsedrawn shadow glaring like devils. The beard inside the buggy like hairs in a nostril. He tries to think of the good life these people lead, of the way they keep clear of all this phony business, this twentieth-century vitamin racket, but in his head they stay devils, risking getting killed trotting along with one dim pink reflector behind, hating Rabbit and his kind, with their big furry tail lights. Who they think they were? He can't shake them, mentally. They never appeared in his rear-view mirror. He passed them and there was nothing. It was just that one sideways glance; the woman's face a hatchet of smoke in the square shadow. Tall coffin lined with hair clopping along to the tune of a dying horse. . . .

The rich earth seems to cast its darkness upward into the air. The farm country is somber at night. He is grateful when the lights of Lancaster merge with his dim beams. He stops at a diner whose clock says 8:04. He hadn't intended to eat until he got out of the state. He takes a map from the rack by the door and while eating three hamburgers at the counter studies his position. He is in Lancaster, surrounded by funny names, Bird in Hand, Paradise, Intercourse, Mt. Airy, Mascot. They probably didn't seem funny if you lived in them.

In the golden age of American musicals after the Second World War when the Broadway stage was alive with the works of Cole Porter, Rodgers and Hammerstein, and Irving Berlin, *Plain and Fancy*, with music by Arnold Horwitt and a book by Joseph Stein and Will Glickman, opened on Broadway January 27, 1955, and had a very respectable run of 461 performances, closing on March 3, 1956. *Plain and Fancy* was a sweet, wholesome, but slightly naughty musical typical of its time, but featuring a New York couple being stranded in Lancaster County surrounded with a large cast of characters with names like "Abner Zook" and "Levi Stolftzfus." The humor was quaint. Two Amish girls are unpacking the New York woman's clothes when they come across a bra. Holding it upside down by the straps one asks the other, "What's this for?" The other answers, "To hold things, I guess?" Big laugh from the audience. The first act finale was, of course, a barn raising.

In the 1980s, a group of tourist promoters revived *Plain and Fancy* in a venue on the Route 30 tourist strip, hoping to turn it into a tourist must-see, like the Radio City Rockettes at Christmas time, but their effort died. The production was chintzy and the times not right.

In the 1968 movie, *The Night they Raided Minsky's*, Norman Lear and William Friedkin presented a comical look at the death of a burlesque in New York City in the 1930s. The backstage aura was given a humorous twist because burlesque entrepreneur Billy Minsky's protégée was innocent Rachel Schititendavel from "Smoketown, PA." There is a hilarious Keystone Kops–like routine with Rachel, the Dutch maid turned stripper; her befuddled, presumably Amish father who arrives to take her back to the farm; Billy Minsky; and the New York police. At the end of the film, Rachel (played by Britt Ekland) is not going back to the farm—nor will she continue as a stripper.

The most commercially successful and satisfying Dutch film to date has been *Witness*, a 1985 movie that was actually filmed in Lancaster County with significant attention to accuracy. It is essentially, like *Plain and Fancy* before it, a fish-out-of-water story. Amish Rachel Lapp, recently widowed, and her son Samuel, are on their way via train to visit her sister in Baltimore. Arriving in Philadelphia, they learn that the train to Baltimore is delayed into the night. In the men's rest room, young Samuel, about age six, witnesses a murder. The police are called in with the lead detective being John Book (played by Harrison Ford). As the plot twists, Book learns that the murder involves narcotics and ultimately his colleagues in the police. Wounded in an assassination attempt by his crooked police brethren, Book secrets Rachel and her son back to the farm where she lives with her father-in-law, Eli.

The movie now places Book in the Amish world. For the sake of keeping the police away, Book is treated by an Amish healer. As he recovers, a romance develops between him and Rachel, which is almost consummated, but isn't, because each realizes that he or she could not live in the other's world.

Book has temporarily entered the Amish sphere, a close-knit community in which gossip is rife. It is also a world of 4:30 a.m. breakfasts, chores, and ribald farmyard humor. When plain-garbed Rachel (played by Kelly McGillis) complains that the English (the outside) world considers them (the Amish) quaint, Book responds ironically, "I wonder why?"

THE PENNSYLVANIA DUTCH COUNTRY

There are many insights into Amish culture and a truly wonderful, if inevitable, barn raising. When Book is well enough to go to town to telephone his partner in Philadelphia, he is dressed as an Amishman, but his attitude is still very "English." He is riding home in a buggy driven by Eli Lapp when some young urban thugs start bullying the Amish. The Amish try to calm him, saying, "do nothing. It's our way." "But it's not my way," he says, as he breaks the nose of one of the taunters. When the inevitable fight takes place with the bad guys, it is in and around the farm where Book's newfound knowledge is an advantage, as is the support of the whole community who come running when young Samuel rings a warning bell.

As Book drives away at the end, as he must, Eli Lapp, who has grudgingly come to respect him, yells out, "Be careful out there, Book, among those English."

Lyrically filmed in Lancaster County, the "Witness Farm" where it was made is now a registered landmark. The barn raised in the film was torn down after filming and the lumber sold at auction. The film was widely debated among Lancaster people, some of whom could not accept the romance between Book and Rachel. The film gave a boost to the local tourist industry, but the effect has largely dissipated over time.

The success of *Witness* did not lead to a spate of Dutch films. Perhaps the most interesting film influenced by *Witness* was *A Stranger Among Us*, in which a female New York City detective (Melanie Griffith) goes undercover to find a murderer in the Brooklyn Hasidic community and falls in love with a Hasid. Does it sound familiar? There have also been several films in subsequent years featuring Amish in silly comedies, but these have all been trivial, with the best of the bad lot being 1996's *Kingpin*, about an Amishman with great bowling talent starring Bill Murray and Randy Quaid.

In *Witness*, the "great popular Amish movie" has possibly been made. There has never been even a mediocre movie about the church people—and it is unlikely that there ever will be. They are too hard to characterize. The *Witness* influence still limps on and was part of the plot of an episode of the television series, *Judging Amy*, broadcast first on November 23, 2003, and featuring Rachel Beiler in a conflict between the Dutch and the English worlds.

All these works—books, plays, and movies—present insights into the larger Dutch world that remains both foreign and familiar—and uniquely American.

BIBLIOGRAPHY

Bach, Jeff. *Voices of the Turtledoves: The Sacred Music of Ephrata.* University Park, Pennsylvania: The Pennsylvania State University Press, 2003.

Brunner, Raymond J. *That Ingenious Business: Pennsylvania German Organ Builders.* Birdsboro, Pennsylvania: The Pennsylvania German Society, 1990.

Bucher, Robert C. "The Continental Log House." *Pennsylvania Folklife 12*, no. 4 (Summer 1962): 18–25.

——————. "Grain in the Attic." *Pennsylvania Folklife 13*, no. 2 (Winter 1962 1963): 7–15.

——————. "The Long Shingle." *Pennsylvania Folklife 18*, no. 9 (Summer 1969): 51–56.

——————. "Steep Roofs and Red Tiles." *Pennsylvania Folklife 12*, no. 2 (Winter 1961–1962): 18–25.

——————. "The Swiss Bank House in Pennsylvania." *Pennsylvania Folklife 18*, no. 2 (Winter 1968-1969): 2–11.

Bucher, Robert C., and Alan G. Keyser. "Thatching in Pennsylvania." *Der Reggeboge 16*, no. 1 (1982): 1–23.

Buffington, Albert F., et al. *Ebbes Fer Alle-Ebber Ebbes Fer Dich.* Breinigsville, Pennsylvania: Pennsylvania German Society, 1980.

Downard, William L. *Dictionary of the History of the American Brewing and Distilling Industries.* Westport, Connecticut: Greenwood Press, 1979.

Earnest, Corinne and Russell D. Earnest. *Fraktur: Folk Art and Family.* Atglen, Pennsylvania: Schiffer Publishing, Ltd., 1997.

Emsminger, Robert F. *The Pennsylvania Barn: Its Origin, Evolution and Destruction in North America.* Baltimore: The Johns Hopkins University Press, 1992.

Expressions of Common Hands: Folk Art of the Pennsylvania Germans. 1998. Produced by New River Media. 90 min. Time Warner Cable. Videocassette.

Fabian, Monroe H. *The Pennsylvania German Decorated Chest.* New York: Main Street Press, 1978.

Faill, Carol E. *Fraktur: A Selective Guide to the Franklin and Marshall Fraktur Collection.* Lancaster, Pennsylvania: Franklin and Marshall College, 1987.

Flowers, Malton D. *Three Cumberland County Wood Carvers: Schimmel, Mountz, Barrett.* Carlisle, Pennsylvania: Cumberland County Historical Society, 1986.

Frederick, J. George. *Pennsylvania Dutch Cook Book.* New York: Dover Publications, Inc., 1971. Reprint of 1935 edition.

Garvin, Beatrice B. *The Pennsylvania German Collection.* Philadelphia: Philadelphia Museum of Art, 1982. Reprint 1999.

Garvin, Beatrice B. and Charles F. Hummel. *The Pennsylvania Germans: A Celebration of their Arts, 1683–1850.* Philadelphia: Philadelphia Museum of Art, 1982.

Gehret, Ellen J. *This is the Way I Pass My Time.* Birdsboro, Pennsylvania: The Pennsylvania German Society, 1985.

Gladfelter, Charles H. *Pennsylvania Germans: A Brief Account of Their Influence on Pennsylvania.* University Park, Pennsylvania: Pennsylvania Historical and Museum Commission, 1990.

Herr, Donald M. *Pewter in Pennsylvania German Churches.* Birdsboro, Pennsylvania: The Pennsylvania German Society, 1995.

Herr, Patricia T. *Amish Arts of Lancaster County.* Atglen, Pennsylvania: Schiffer Publishing, Ltd., 1998.

Hess, Clarke E. *Mennonite Arts.* Atglen, Pennsylvania: Schiffer Publishing, Ltd., 2002.

Historic Preservation Trust of Lancaster County. *Lancaster County Architecture, 1700–1850.* Lancaster, Pennsylvania: Intelligencer Printing Company, 1992.

Hopf, Claudia. *Scherenschnitte: Traditional Paper Cutting.* Lebanon, Pennsylvania: Applied Arts, 1977.

Hostetler, John A. *Amish Society.* Baltimore: The Johns Hopkins University Press, 1963.

Hunter, William Frederick. *Stiegel Glass.* New York: Dover Publications, 1950. Reprint of 1914 edition.

Hutson-Saxton, Martha Y. *Walter Emerson Baum, 1884–1956: Pennsylvania Artist and Founder of the Baum School of Art and the Allentown Art Museum.* Allentown, Pennsylvania: Allentown Art Museum, 1996.

Index of American Design. *Pennsylvania German Folk Art: From the Index of*

Bibliography

American Design. Washington, D.C.: National Gallery of Art, *c.* 1996.

Kauffman, Henry. *Pennsylvania Dutch: American Folk Art.* New York: Dover Publications, Inc., 1964.

Kindig, Joe Jr. *Thoughts on the Kentucky Rifle in Its Golden Age.* York, Pennsylvania: Trimmer Printing, Inc., 1960.

Klein, Georges. *Le Musée Alsacien de Strasbourg.* Strasbourg, France: Musées de Strasbourg, 1970.

Lasansky, Jeannette. *Made of Mud: Stoneware Potteries in Central Pennsylvania, 1834–1929.* Lewisburg, Pennsylvania: Union County Bicentennial Commission, 1977.

——————. *Pieced by Mother: Over 100 Years of Quiltmaking Traditions.* Lewisburg, Pennsylvania: Oral Traditions Project, 1987.

——————. *To Draw, Upset, and Weld: The Work of the Pennsylvania Rural Blacksmith, 1742–1935.* State College, Pennsylvania: Pennsylvania State University, 1980.

——————. *Willow, Oak & Rye: Basket Traditions in Pennsylvania.* Lewisburg, Pennsylvania: Union County Oral Traditions Project, 1978.

Leach, MacEdward and Henry H. Glassie. *A Guide for Collectors of Oral Traditions and Folk Cultural Material in Pennsylvania.* Harrisburg, Pennsylvania: Pennsylvania Historical and Museum Commission, 1968.

Long, Amos, Jr. *The Pennsylvania German Family Farm.* Breinigsville, Pennsylvania: The Pennsylvania German Society, 1972.

Machmer, Richard S. and Rosemarie B. Machmer. *Just for Nice: Carving and Whittling Magic of Southeastern Pennsylvania.* Reading, Pennsylvania: Historical Society of Berks County, 1991.

Martin, Helen R. *Tillie, A Mennonite Maid: A Story of the Pennsylvania Dutch.* Reprint. Ridgewood, New Jersey: Gregg Press, 1968.

Mercer, Henry C. *The Bible in Iron.* Doylestown, Pennsylvania: Bucks County Historical Society, 1961.

Michener, James A. *Centennial.* New York: Random House, 1974.

Moyer, Dennis K. *Fraktur Writings and Folk Art Drawings of the Schwenkfelder Library Collection.* Kutztown, Pennsylvania: The Pennsylvania German Society, 1997.

Murtaugh, William J. *Moravian Architecture and Town Planning: Bethlehem*

Pennsylvania and Other Eighteenth Century Settlements in America. Chapel Hill, North Carolina: The University of North Carolina Press, 1967.

Nolt, Steven M. *Foreigners in Their Own Land: Pennsylvania Germans in the Early Republic*. University Park, Pennsylvania: The Pennsylvania State University Press, 2002.

O'Hara, John. *A Rage to Live*. New York: Random House, 1949.

——————. *Appointment in Samara*. Reprint. New York: New American Library, 1953.

——————. *Ten North Frederick*. New York: Random House, 1955.

Richman, Irwin. *German Architecture in America: Folk House, Your House, Bauhaus, and More*. Atglen, Pennsylvania: Schiffer Publishing, Ltd., 2003.

——————. *Pennsylvania German Arts: More Than Heats, Parrots and Tulips*. Atglen, Pennsylvania: Schiffer Publishing, Ltd., 2001.

——————. "The Pennsylvania-German Foursquare Garden." *The Magazine Antiques*. July 2001, 92–97.

Robacker, Earl F. *Pennsylvania Dutch Stuff: A Guide to Country Antiques*. Philadelphia: University of Pennsylvania Press, 1944.

Steigerwalt, Pansy Nee Hinger, Comp. *The Steigerwalt Family, 1767–1979*. 3rd ed. Hazleton, Pennsylvania: Transnational Printing and Copy Center, 1980.

Shoemaker, Alfred A. *Christmas in Pennsylvania: A Folk Cultural Study*. Reprint ed. Harrisburg, Pennsylvania: Stackpole Books, 1999.

——————. *Easter Tide in Pennsylvania: A Folk Cultural Study*. Kutztown, Pennsylvania: Pennsylvania German Folklife Society, 1960.

Snyder, John J. "C. Emlen Urban: A Reconsideration." *Susquehanna Magazine*, April 1982, 28–31.

Updike, John. *Rabbit, Run*. New York: Alfred A. Knopf, 1960.

Weaver, William Woys. *Pennsylvania Dutch Country Cooking*. New York: Abbeville Press, 1993.

——————. *Sauerkraut Yankees: Pennsylvania German Foods and Foodways*. Philadelphia: University of Pennsylvania Press, 1983.

Yoder, Don. *Pennsylvania Dutch Barn Symbols and their Meaning*, 2nd ed. Harrisburg, Pennsylvania: Stackpole Books, 2000.

INDEX